Children's *healthy & fun* COOKBOOK

LONDON, NEW YORK, MUNICH,
MELBOURNE AND DELHI

Senior Editor Catherine Saunders
Senior Designer Lisa Crowe
Editor Julia March
Editorial Assistant Elizabeth Noble
Designers Thelma-Jane Robb and Dan Bunyan
DTP Designer Hanna Ländin
Home Economist Denise Smart
Publishing Manager Simon Beecroft
Category Publisher Alex Allan/Siobhan Williamson
Production Amy Bennett

First published in Great Britain in 2007 by
Dorling Kindersley Limited,
80 Strand, London WC2R 0RL

ISBN: 978-1-40531-909-6

Reproduced by Media Development and Printing Ltd., UK
Printed and bound in China by Toppan

Acknowledgements
The publisher would like to thank the photographer's assistants Jon Cardwell and Michael Hart for all their help,
and the following young chefs for working so hard to make this book so healthy *and* fun:
Efia Brady, Ella Bukbardis, Megan Craddock, Eliza Greenslade, George Greenslade, Eva Mee, Grace Mee,
Shannon O'Kelly, Gabriella Soper, Rachel Tilley, Charlotte Vogel and Hope Wadman.

Discover more at
www.dk.com

Children's
healthy & fun
COOKBOOK

Written by Nicola Graimes
Photography by Howard Shooter

Contents

Jacket Potato
See p.35

Strawberry Scrunch
See p.24–25

Fruit Yoghurt
See p.86

Tuna Pasta
See p.58–59

Sunflower Seed Rolls
See p.122–123

Introduction

In this book you'll find out why healthy eating is important and how to make your diet balanced *and* tasty. You will also discover lots of ideas for balanced breakfasts, luscious light meals and mouthwatering main meals, all designed to suit even the fussiest eaters! And don't worry, there are plenty of recipes for desserts, cakes and cookies too – all with a healthy twist.

Getting started

1. Read the recipe thoroughly before you begin.

2. Wash your hands, tie your hair back (if necessary) and put on your apron.

3. Gather all the ingredients and equipment you need before you begin.

4. Start cooking!

Be sensible! Take extra care when you see this symbol because hot ovens, cookers or sharp knives are involved.

You might need to ask an adult for help if you see this symbol. But don't be shy – ask for help whenever you think you need it!

Safe cooking

Cooking is great fun but with heat and sharp objects around, you must always take care to be safe and sensible.

• Use oven gloves when handling hot pans, trays or bowls.

• Don't put hot pans or trays directly onto the work surface – use a heatproof trivet, mat, rack or board.

• When you are stirring food on the cooker, grip the handle firmly to steady the pan.

• When cooking on the stove, turn the pan handles to the side (away from the heat and the front) so that you are less likely to knock them over.

• Take extra care on any step where you see the red warning triangle.

• Ask an adult for help when you see the green warning triangle.

Kitchen hygiene

After safety, cleanliness is the most important thing to be aware of in the kitchen. Here are a few simple hygiene rules for you to follow.

- Always wash your hands before you start cooking and after handling raw meat.
- Wash all fruit and vegetables.
- Use separate chopping boards for meat and vegetables.
- Keep your cooking area clean and have a cloth handy to wipe up any spills.
- Store cooked and raw food separately.
- Always check the use-by date on all ingredients. Do not use them if the date has passed.
- Keep meat and fish in the refrigerator until you need them and always take care to cook them thoroughly.

Did you know?
Humans are the only creatures on Earth that eat cooked food. All other creatures (except for domesticated animals) eat their food raw and unprocessed.

Using the recipes

There is a lot of information to take in so here's how to get the most out of the recipes. They don't just tell you how to cook the food, they suggest alternatives, give helpful advice and provide some amazing facts about the food you eat.

Check out useful cooking tips.

This tells you which section the recipe is from.

Check here for preparation and cooking times.

Discover some amazing food trivia in this box.

All the recipes can be adapted to suit your personal taste.

Learn more about why certain foods are good for you.

Collect all the ingredients and equipment you need before you start.

Step-by-step pictures and text guide you through the recipes.

Fruit and Vegetables

Eating lots of fruit and vegetables is a vital part of a healthy diet and some scientists believe it could actually help you to live longer. Fresh fruit and vegetables may even help to protect you against many of the major diseases found in the modern world, including cancer and heart disease.

You should eat a minimum of five portions of different fruit and vegetables every day. One portion is roughly equal to the amount you can hold in one hand, e.g. 1 apple, a few grapes, 1 orange, 1 kiwi fruit, 1–2 florets of broccoli, a bowl of salad, 1 small corn-on-the-cob and so on.

Why are fruit and vegetables good for you?

Fruit and vegetables are good for you because they provide important vitamins, minerals, fibre and natural plant compounds known as phytochemicals. As well as their health benefits, these phytochemicals are responsible for the colour, taste and smell of a fruit or vegetable.

What doesn't count?

There are a few foods that don't count in the five-a-day guidelines, either because they are too high in starch or do not have a high enough fruit or vegetable content. These are:

- Potatoes, yams and sweet potatoes
- Ketchup and the tomato sauce in beans (although the beans do count)
- Fruit-flavoured drinks, e.g. squash
- Shop-bought fruit yoghurts
- Shop-bought jam or marmalade

Melon Fruit Bowl
p.88-89

I can eat a rainbow...

Fruit and vegetables are a colourful and fun part of any healthy, balanced diet. Different coloured fruit and vegetables provide different nutrients.

Red

Red fruit and vegetables such as tomatoes, sweet peppers, strawberries, grapes and cherries are a great source of vitamin C, which supports the immune system and helps the condition of your skin, hair and nails.

tomatoes

Yellow

The yellow colour of fruit and vegetables such as bananas, sweet peppers, sweetcorn, melon and pineapple comes from carotenoids, which have been found to protect the body against cancer and heart disease.

yellow peppers

Orange

Orange fruit and vegetables such as carrots, pumpkin, squash, mango, apricots and sweet peppers contain large amounts of beta carotene and vitamin C. Beta carotene is great for boosting your immune system and research shows that vitamin C can significantly reduce the length and severity of a cold. If you haven't already, give pumpkin and squash a try because they contain even more beta carotene than a large carrot!

oranges

Green

Broccoli, cabbage and sprouts have all been described as super-vegetables because they are so rich in vitamins and minerals – particularly beta carotene, vitamins B and C, iron, potassium and calcium – that help to support your immune system.

broccoli

Did you know?

It can be difficult to get the right balance but you won't go wrong if you eat a combination of different coloured fruit and vegetables every day – they can be fresh, frozen, tinned or dried.

Purple

Purple fruit and vegetables, such as grapes, aubergines, blackcurrants, blueberries, blackberries, figs, beetroot and red cabbage are an excellent source of vitamin C. They also contain bioflavonoids, which help your body to absorb vitamin C and reduce pain if you bump or bruise yourself.

blueberries

Starchy Foods

Bread, cereals, rice, pasta and potatoes are all starchy foods. They are from the food group known as carbohydrates. These types of food are the body's major source of energy so they should form the main part of every meal. They also contain useful amounts of fibre, vitamins and, perhaps surprisingly, protein. Sugary foods are also a type of carbohydrates. (See p.14–15.)

You should eat 4–6 servings of carbohydrates every day, depending on your age. A serving is 1 piece of bread, a serving of rice or pasta, 1 medium potato or a bowl of breakfast cereal.

Good carbohydrates

Wholemeal pasta

There are lots of different types of starchy foods to choose from but always choose wholegrain varieties if you can. Wholegrain foods contain more vitamins, minerals and fibre than processed foods because many nutrients are lost during the refining process.

brown rice

Bread

The best types of bread are those made from wholegrain flour as they provide B vitamins, vitamin E and fibre. White bread still has some vitamins and minerals but is lacking in fibre. There are plenty of interesting varieties to choose from, including:

- Tortilla
- Pitta
- Bagels
- Soda bread
- Rye bread
- Foccacia
- Ciabatta

Oaty Bread see p.106

Breakfast cereal see p.16

Grains and cereals

Grains have been grown throughout the world for centuries. These seeds of cereal grasses are very versatile and also low in fat:

- **Wheat**
- **Rye**
- **Quinoa**
- **Millet**
- **Buckwheat**
- **Couscous**
- **Bulgur wheat**

Jambalaya see p.76–77

Rice

Rice is popular in many countries throughout the world and forms an important part of diets in India, China and Japan. There are many types to choose from:

- **Long-grain**
- **Short-grain (rice pudding)**
- **Basmati**
- **Arborio (risotto)**
- **Sticky rice (sushi)**

Fibre

Starchy foods are also a good source of dietary fibre, which is only found in foods that come from plants. High fibre foods include wholemeal bread, brown rice, wholemeal pasta and wholegrain breakfast cereals, which mostly contain insoluble fibre. Although the body cannot digest this type of fibre, it helps the passage of other food and waste products through your gut and keeps your bowels working properly. Soluble fibre is found in oats and pulses and can be digested by your body.

oats

Potatoes

There are thousands of potato varieties and certain types are best suited to particular cooking methods such as roasting, boiling or mashing. Vitamins and minerals are found in, or just below, the skin, so it is best to serve potatoes unpeeled or scrubbed, if you can. The skin is also the best source of fibre.

potatoes

Protein

There are lots of different types of foods in this group and protein is found in both animal and plant sources. Protein is made up of amino acids, which are essential for building you up and keeping you strong. Try to get your protein from a wide range of foods for a balanced and varied diet.

Eat 2–4 servings a day. A serving could be a handful of nuts and seeds, 1 egg or a serving of meat, fish or pulses (beans, peas, lentils).

Meat

Meat is a good source of vitamins and minerals such as iron, zinc, selenium and B vitamins but it can also be high in saturated fat (see p.14–15). It is best to choose lean cuts of meat or cut off excess fat before cooking. Poultry is lower in fat than red meat, especially if the skin is removed.

Types of red meat:
- Beef
- Pork
- Lamb
- Venison

Types of poultry:
- Chicken
- Turkey
- Duck

Lamb Kebabs
See p. 68-69

Tofu and eggs are two valuable sources of protein. Tofu also provides calcium, iron, and vitamins B1, B2 and B3 (see p.48-49 and 78-79), while eggs contain B vitamins, iron, calcium and zinc (see p.31 and 41).

tofu

Nuts and seeds

Nuts and seeds are a good source of protein and also provide a rich collection of vitamins, minerals and 'good' fats such as omega-6 (see p.14–15). However, because they are high in fat, you shouldn't eat too many and you should especially try to avoid salted nuts.

Types of nuts and seeds:
- Peanuts
- Brazil nuts
- Walnuts
- Cashews
- Hazelnuts
- Almonds
- Sunflower seeds
- Sesame seeds
- Pumpkin seeds
- Poppy seeds
- Linseeds

Fish

You should eat at least two portions of fish a week, including one of oily fish. Salmon, tuna, sardines, mackerel, trout and herring are all types of oily fish that are rich in omega-3 fats (see p.14–15) as well as protein.

Salmon Parcels
see p.70–71

Pulses

A pulse is an edible seed that grows in a pod. As well as being a good source of protein, they are low in fat and also contain significant amounts of carbohydrates. Tinned pulses are quick and easy to use but try to buy products without added sugar and salt.

Popular pulses:
- Lentils
- Dried peas
- Chickpeas
- Haricot beans
- Flageolet beans
- Cannellini beans
- Kidney beans
- Soya beans

Did you know?
A fried chicken breast in breadcrumbs contains nearly 6 times as much fat as a grilled skinless chicken breast.

Dairy

As well as protein, dairy produce also provides valuable vitamins and minerals, such as calcium and vitamins A, B12 and D.

milk

Yoghurt Swirl with Dippers
see p. 26–27

Types of dairy
- Milk
- Yoghurt
- Cheese
- Butter
- Fromage frais
- Cream
- Crème fraîche
- Buttermilk

Alternatives to dairy
- Fortified breakfast cereals
- Soya milk
- Tofu
- Green leafy vegetables
- Molasses
- Tinned sardines
- Baked beans
- Sea vegetables
- Sesame seeds

Eat 2–3 servings of calcium-rich foods a day for strong bones and teeth. A serving equals a glass of milk, a pot of yoghurt or a small portion of cheese.

Fats and Sugars

You need some fat in your diet because it provides your body with lots of energy, helps it to absorb some vitamins and provides essential fatty acids, such as omega-3 and omega-6. But it is important to eat the right types such as polyunsaturated and monounsaturated and to try and avoid saturated and trans fats.

Be careful not to eat too much fat. A good way to check how much fat your food contains is to look at the label. 20g (¾ oz) of fat per 100g (3½ oz) of food is a lot of fat; and 3g (1/10 oz) or less of fat per 100g (3½ oz) is a little fat. Use what you learn in this book to be sensible about your fat intake.

chips

croissants

cheese

Bad fats

Saturated and trans fats are generally solid at room temperature and are primarily from animal sources (except fish). They are found in lard, butter, hard margarine, cheese, whole milk and anything that contains these ingredients, such as cakes, chocolate, biscuits, pies and pastries. Saturated fat is also the white fat you can see on red meat and underneath poultry skin. The less saturated fat you eat, the better it is for your health – a high fat intake has been linked with an increased risk of coronary heart disease.

cake

avocadoes

olive oil

Good fats

Unsaturated fats (polyunsaturated and monounsaturated) are usually liquid at room temperature. They are a much healthier alternative to saturated fat, helping to fuel the body, transport nutrients around the body and also to protect your heart. Unsaturated fats generally come from vegetable sources (and some fish). These sources include vegetable oils such as sesame, sunflower, soya and olive plus nuts, seeds, avocadoes and oily fish, such as mackerel, sardines, pilchards and salmon; and soft margarine. However, although these fats are healthy you only need a small amount to get the health benefits you need.

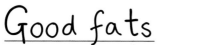
sunflower seeds

hazelnuts

fish

Some simple ways to cut down on bad fats

- Snack on unsalted nuts and seeds instead of biscuits and crisps.
- Spread mashed avocado or houmous on toast instead of butter.
- Choose oily fish instead of battered fish or meat pies.
- For a change, mash olive oil into potatoes instead of butter.
- Drizzle olive oil and lemon juice over salads in place of creamy salad dressings.
- Nibble fresh or dried fruit rather than biscuits and chocolate.
- Trim any visible fat off meat and poultry.
- Buy lean cuts of meat and reduced-fat mince.
- Ditch the frying pan – try poaching, steaming, grilling or baking.
  - Swap whole milk for semi-skimmed or skimmed alternatives.
  - If you use lard, butter or hard margarine, switch to plant-based oils and low-fat spreads.

raisins

raspberries

strawberries

houmous

jam

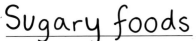
Sugary foods

crisps

Like fat, sugar is a concentrated source of energy. It is found in foods such as jam, sweets, cakes, chocolate, soft drinks, biscuits and ice cream. The psychological benefits of eating these foods are obvious – they taste lovely! However, too much sugar causes tooth decay, obesity and mood swings so it is important to limit your intake.

lollies

fizzy drink

Salt

Eating too much salt is linked to high blood pressure, heart disease and strokes. It's not just obvious foods such as crisps and salted peanuts that contain salt, it is also hiding in breakfast cereals, bread, cakes and biscuits. This means that it can be very difficult to tell if you are eating too much so check your food labels first to see if salt has been added. When it comes to adding salt at the table, it is easy to get into the habit of using too much. Always taste your food before reaching for the salt pot – you will find that your food tastes fine without it.

salt

Breakfasts

After a night's sleep you need fuel – a good breakfast to prepare you for the day ahead. Foods high in carbohydrates, such as cereals and bread, are ideal for breakfast because they are broken down into glucose which fuels your brain. Protein foods such as yoghurt, milk, eggs, bacon, sausages and beans are important, too. They control your body's growth and development, and boost alertness. There are lots of tasty recipes in this section and here are some simple ideas to get you started.

Boiled Egg
Half-fill a small saucepan with water. Gently lower an egg into the pan and bring the water to the boil. Boil the egg for 4 minutes, then remove it with a slotted spoon. Dip the egg in cold water and place it in an egg cup. Carefully slice the top off the egg and serve with toast.

Naturally Sweet
Shop-bought cereals can be very high in sugar. Buy sugar-free wheat or oat flakes instead, and add your favourite combination of dried fruit, nuts or seeds.

Quick and Easy
Give energy levels a quick boost. Simply add sliced banana, a dollop of natural bio yoghurt and a drizzle of honey to wholemeal seedy toast or fruit bread.

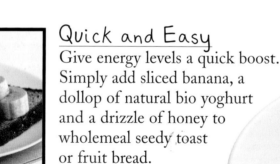

Add Fruit!
Start the day in a super-healthy way by adding fresh fruit to your breakfast cereal. It provides vitamins and natural sweetness.

Stewed Apple (serves 4)

Peel and core 4 apples, then chop them into bite-sized pieces. Put them into a saucepan and add 1 tsp ground cinnamon, 4 tbsp apple juice and a squeeze of lemon juice. Half-cover the pan and simmer for 15–20 minutes or until the apples are tender. Serve with a fruit muffin or stirred into yoghurt.

Cooked Breakfast

Treat yourself to a cooked breakfast once in a while, but grill instead of fry it. Use lean meat or vegetarian sausages and add grilled tomatoes, mushrooms, wholemeal toast and scrambled eggs for a balanced breakfast.

Poached Egg

Fill a pan with water (about 5cm/2in deep) and bring it to a simmer. Crack an egg into a cup. Swirl the water in the pan and then gently pour the egg into the centre of the pan. Cook for 3 minutes or until the white is set and the yolk is slightly runny. Scoop out using a slotted spoon and serve with wholemeal toast.

Porridge (serves 4)

Put 200g (7oz) porridge oats in a saucepan with 250ml (9fl oz) milk and 250ml (9fl oz) water. Bring to the boil, then reduce the heat and simmer, stirring, for about 4 minutes or until creamy and smooth.

Fruit Salad

Fruit salads are perfect for breakfast, dessert or as a healthy snack. Use a combination of your favourite fruit. Bio yoghurt also tastes great with this recipe.

Boost Nutrients

A sprinkling of seeds or chopped nuts will boost the nutritional content of porridge and other breakfast cereals as well as adding extra flavour.

Carrot and Apple Juice

This fresh juice is bursting with vitamin C! Don't worry if you don't have a juicer, just remove the apple cores and make a purée using a blender or food processor. Then use a sieve to separate the juice from the pulp.

For maximum goodness, drink the juice immediately.

Healthy Hint
The lemon juice helps to preserve the vitamins in the juice and also brings out the flavour of the apple and carrot.

Ingredients
● 4 apples
● 3 carrots
● squeeze of fresh lemon juice (optional)

Equipment
● small sharp knife
● chopping board
● juicer

juicer

1 Scrub the carrots and cut each one into 2 or 3 pieces. Remove the stalks from the apples and carefully cut them into quarters.

2 Put the apples and carrots through the juicer. Throw away the pulp and pour the juice into two glasses. Add a squeeze of lemon juice and stir the juice.

Fruit Smoothie

This creamy drink will give you plenty of energy for the day ahead – and it's so easy to make! Serve it with cereal or toast for a complete breakfast.

Tasty Twist

Swap the blueberries for the same weight of strawberries for a classic combination.

Ingredients

- 150g (5½ oz) fresh or frozen blueberries
- 3 bananas (sliced)
- 1 tsp vanilla extract (optional)
- 500g ml (17 fl oz) thick natural bio yoghurt
- 200ml (7fl oz) milk

banana   blueberries

Equipment

- small sharp knife
- chopping board
- blender

chopping board

1 Peel the bananas and then roughly chop them into small slices. Put them into the blender and add the blueberries, vanilla extract, yoghurt and milk.

2 Whiz in the blender until the mixture is smooth, thick and creamy. Pour the smoothie into four tall glasses and enjoy this simple and nutritious breakfast.

Fruit and Nut Bars

This homemade version of a fruit cereal bar is packed with energy-giving apricots, raisins, nuts and seeds. It makes an excellent start to the day, especially with a calcium-rich glass of milk or pot of yoghurt. It could also be a healthy addition to a lunchbox.

Tasty Twists

Any type of ready-to-eat dried fruit can be used to make these bars. Why not experiment with pre-mixed bags, such as tropical fruit or fruits of the forest?

Ingredients

- 50g (2oz) hazelnuts
- 50g (2oz) whole oats
- 100g (3½ oz) raisins
- 150g (5½ oz) dried apricots (cut into small pieces)
- 4 tbsp fresh orange juice
- 2 tbsp sunflower seeds
- 2 tbsp pumpkin seeds

raisins

pumpkin seeds

sunflower seeds

oats

Equipment

- frying pan
- wooden spatula
- small sharp knife
- chopping board
- food processor or blender
- large mixing bowl
- greaseproof paper
- palette knife
- 18cm x 25cm (7in x 10in) tin

palette knife

1 Put the hazelnuts, oats and seeds into a frying pan. Dry fry, stirring, over a medium heat for 3 mins, or until they begin to turn golden. Leave to cool.

2 Put the raisins, apricots and orange juice into a food processor and purée until the mixture becomes smooth. Pour the purée into a mixing bowl.

3 Put the nuts, oats and seeds in the food processor and whiz until they are finely chopped. Tip the mixture into the bowl with the fruit purée.

Cut into 8–10 slices and eat as part of a nutritious breakfast.

Did you know?
Hazelnuts are high in fibre, potassium, calcium, magnesium and vitamin E so they are nutritious as well as tasty!

Food Facts
Drying fruit is one of the oldest methods of preserving. The drying process concentrates the nutrients making dried fruit a useful source of fibre, natural sugars, vitamins B and C, iron, calcium and other minerals. However, levels of vitamin C are lower than in fresh fruit.

dried apricots

4 Stir the fruit mixture until all the ingredients are mixed together. Line a 18cm x 25cm (7in x 10in) baking tin with greaseproof paper.

5 Spread the fruit mixture evenly in the tin. Chill for at least 1 hour, or until solid. Turn it out of the tin and peel off the greaseproof paper. Cut into bars.

Mixed Fruit Puff

Shop-bought cereals can be full of unnecessary sugar but this healthier version relies on the natural sweetness of the dried fruit, which is also full of fibre and nutrients such as iron. Just add milk for a delicious and nutritious breakfast.

Tasty Twists

Any mixture of your favourite fruits and nuts can be used in this recipe. For a different texture, you could swap the puffed rice for oats to make muesli. Or try serving the cereal with a tasty topping of fresh fruit.

Ingredients

- 75g (3oz) whole hazelnuts
- 8 tbsp sunflower seeds
- 125g (4½ oz) dried apricots (cut into small pieces)
- 250g (9oz) sugar-free puffed rice cereal
- 125g (4½ oz) raisins
- 50g (2oz) flaked coconut

hazelnuts

puffed rice cereal

dried apricots

Equipment

- frying pan
- wooden spoon
- small bowl
- freezer bag
- rolling pin
- kitchen scissors
- mixing bowl

rolling pin

frying pan

Did you know?

More than 10 billion pints of milk are sold every year in Great Britain and over 25% of that milk is consumed with tea.

1 Put the nuts in a frying pan and dry fry over a medium-low heat. Use a wooden spoon to turn the nuts and cook for 3 mins, or until they begin to turn golden.

2 Pour the nuts into a bowl and leave them to cool. Put the sunflower seeds in the frying pan and fry them for 2 mins. They should be golden but not burnt.

3 Leave the sunflower seeds to cool. Pour the cooled nuts into a small plastic food bag. Fold over the open end and hold it closed with one hand.

Storing the cereal in an airtight container will keep it fresh for longer.

Food Facts

Nuts and seeds provide a nutritious combination of B vitamins, iron, vitamin E, and zinc, plus omega-6 fats, which are important for brain function and energy levels. Sunflower seeds help to keep your immune system strong as they provide zinc, magnesium and selenium. Their vitamin E content helps to keep skin healthy.

sunflower seeds

4 Using your other hand, bash the nuts with the rolling pin until they are broken into small pieces. Then cut the apricots into small pieces.

5 Put the puffed rice cereal into a large mixing bowl. Add the apricots, nuts, seeds, raisins and coconut and gently mix together with your hands.

Strawberry Scrunch

Toasted oats and seeds make this layered breakfast a crunchy treat, and provide important nutrients too. The yoghurt is a low-fat source of protein and calcium, while the strawberries and orange juice are rich in vitamin C. Honey adds natural sweetness, but you could use maple syrup instead.

Tasty Twists

Swap strawberries for your favourite fruits such as bananas, nectarines or peaches. Fruit purée also tastes great! (See p.26–27 and 86.)

Ingredients

- 150g (5½ oz) strawberries (about 6-8)
- 4 tbsp fresh orange juice
- 50g (2oz) whole porridge oats
- 3 tbsp sunflower seeds
- 3 tbsp pumpkin seeds
- 2-3 tbsp clear runny honey
- 12 dsp thick natural bio yoghurt

pumpkin seeds

honey

strawberries

Equipment

- small sharp knife
- chopping board
- small bowl
- frying pan
- wooden spoon

chopping board

1 Cut the green stalks and leaves from the strawberries and then thickly slice the fruit. Put the strawberries in a bowl and add the orange juice. Set aside.

2 Put the oats in a frying pan and dry fry over a medium-low heat for 3 mins. Turn the oats occasionally with a wooden spoon to make sure they cook evenly.

3 Add the sunflower and pumpkin seeds and dry fry for another 2 minutes or until light golden. Take care – the pumpkin seeds may pop a little!

This would also make a great-tasting dessert!

Food Facts

Oats are a carbohydrate food. They are perfect for breakfast because the fibre in them is digested by the body slowly. This makes you feel full for longer and keeps your blood sugar levels steady. Oats are also a great source of vitamins E, B1 and B2.

oats

4 Take the pan off the heat. Stir in the honey – it will sizzle at first but keep stirring until the oats and seeds are coated. Allow to cool slightly.

5 Put a layer of the oats in the bottom of each glass. Add 2 heaped dessert spoonfuls of yoghurt and then some of the fruit. Add another layer of each.

Yoghurt Swirl with Dippers

Unlike shop-bought yoghurts, you won't find refined sugar or additives in this recipe. Instead these tasty yoghurts are low in fat, high in calcium, protein and potassium and have a swirl of vitamin-rich dried fruit. Have fun dipping the toasted fruit bread fingers into your breakfast!

Tasty Twists

Fresh fruit or fruit purées are also good mixed into yoghurt. Try mango, strawberry, raspberry or stewed apples. (See p.17 and 86.)

Ingredients

- 100g (3½ oz) dried dates or apricots (chopped)
- 250ml (9fl oz) water
- 3 tbsp fresh apple juice
- 500g (1lb 2oz) thick natural bio yoghurt
- 4-8 slices raisin bread

dried dates

dried apricots

Equipment

- medium saucepan with lid
- blender
- spoon
- 4 bowls

1 Put the dates or apricots and water in the saucepan. Bring to the boil and then reduce the heat to low. Cover, and cook the fruit for 15-20 mins, or until soft.

Fruit muffins or bagels could also be dipped!

Food Facts

Bio yoghurt contains beneficial bacteria that are thought to help boost your immune system, help your digestive system and fight off infection.

bio yoghurt

Did you know?

Yoghurt has been around since ancient times. The word itself originates from the Turkish language.

2 Leave the dates or apricots to cool for about 30 minutes and then stir in the apple juice. Spoon the mixture into a blender and whiz until smooth.

3 Divide the yoghurt between four bowls. Put 2 tablespoons of the fruit purée on top of each serving and then stir gently to make a swirled pattern.

4 Toast the raisin bread until it is light golden. Cut the toast into narrow strips and dip them into the yoghurt mixture. Delicious!

Banana Pancakes

These American-style pancakes make a tasty and nutritious brunch when served with summer berries and a drizzle of maple syrup. Fruit sauce (see p.86) and yoghurt would also taste delicious.

Helpful Hint

It is important that the batter is free from lumps. If you do get lumps in your batter, press it through a sieve using the back of a spoon.

Ingredients

- 100g (3½ oz) self-raising flour
- 40g (1½ oz) self-raising wholemeal flour
- 2 tbsp caster sugar
- 1 free-range egg
- 175ml (6fl oz) milk
- 2 bananas (peeled)
- butter (for frying)

egg

wholemeal flour

sieve

Equipment

- sieve
- 2 mixing bowls
- wooden spoon
- jug
- whisk or fork
- large non-stick frying pan
- ladle
- spatula
- masher or fork

ladle

mixing bowl

1 Sieve both types of flour into a mixing bowl, adding any bran left in the sieve. Stir in the sugar and make a well in the centre of the mixture.

2 Measure the milk in a jug and then crack the egg straight into it. Lightly beat the egg and milk with a fork or whisk until they are mixed together.

3 Pour the egg mixture into the well in the centre of the flour and sugar. Beat with a wooden spoon until you have a smooth, creamy batter.

4 Leave the batter to rest for about 30 minutes – this will make the pancakes lighter. Mash the bananas in a bowl then stir them into the rested batter.

Food Facts

Choose ripe bananas when making these pancakes – they are not only easier to mash but also their nutrients (vitamins B and C, potassium, iron and beta carotene) are more easily absorbed by the body. Under-ripe bananas are more difficult to digest and can give you stomach ache.

bananas

Did you know?

In France pancakes are known as 'crêpes', in Russia they are called 'blinis' and in Latin America they are called 'panqueques'.

5 Heat a small knob of butter in a frying pan. Add 3 small ladlefuls of batter to make 3 pancakes, each one about 8cm (3¼in) in diameter.

6 Cook for 2 mins, or until bubbles appear on the surface. Flip the pancakes over and cook for another 2 minutes, so both sides are light golden.

7 Keep the cooked pancakes warm in a low oven while you cook more pancakes with the rest of the batter, adding a little knob of butter between each batch.

Egg Cups

Eggs are a great source of high quality protein – ideal for kick-starting your day! This recipe is perfect for a filling weekend brunch or even a light meal.

Helpful Hint

Timing and temperature are really important when cooking scrambled eggs. If they are cooked for too long over too high a heat, the eggs become dry and crumbly.

Did you know?

The type of hen determines the colour of the egg shell. Those with white feathers and ear lobes lay white eggs and those with red feathers and ear lobes lay brown eggs.

Ingredients

- 4 crusty rolls
- 3 tomatoes (optional)
- 8 free-range eggs
- 5 tbsp milk
- salt and pepper
- 50g (2oz) unsalted butter

crusty rolls

tomatoes

Equipment

- sharp knife
- chopping board
- mixing bowl
- whisk or fork
- medium saucepan

whisk

chopping board

1 Slice the tops off the rolls and then use your fingers to scoop out the centre of each one. (The insides can be used to make breadcrumbs.)

2 Cut the tomatoes in half and scoop out the seeds with a teaspoon. Then slice the deseeded tomatoes into small, bite-sized pieces.

Food Facts

Eggs are one of the most nutritious foods and make a valuable contribution to your diet. They contain B vitamins, iron, calcium and zinc, as well as protein. However, four eggs per week is the maximum recommended intake as they are high in cholesterol. The eggs of many different types of birds can be eaten, but those of the female chicken (hen) are most widely available.

eggs

3 Crack each egg into a mixing bowl by tapping it firmly against the side, pushing your thumbs into the crack and pulling the shell apart.

4 Add the milk to the bowl. Whisk the eggs and milk together using a fork or small hand whisk. Season the mixture with a little salt and pepper.

5 Put the butter into the saucepan and melt it over a medium to low heat. When the butter begins to bubble, add the tomatoes and cook for 1 minute.

6 Pour in the egg mixture. Stir gently to prevent the egg sticking to the pan. Continue for 3 minutes or until the eggs are firm. Remove from the heat.

7 Spoon a serving of scrambled egg and tomatoes into each roll. Balance the roll lids on top and serve. A glass of orange juice is the perfect accompaniment.

Breakfast Tortilla

A tortilla is a thick, flat omelette and is a popular dish in Spain. This is a twist on the classic combination of eggs, onion and potatoes and makes a filling breakfast or a tasty light meal.

Did you know?
'Tortilla' is the Spanish word for omelette. In Italy it is called 'frittata'. However, in Mexico, 'tortilla' means a thin (unleavened) bread usually made from corn.

Ingredients

- 4 good quality sausages (or vegetarian alternative)
- 4 medium-sized potatoes (peeled, cooked and left to cool)
- 2 tbsp sunflower oil

eggs

- 8 cherry tomatoes (halved)
- 5 eggs (lightly beaten)
- salt and pepper

potatoes

cherry tomatoes

Equipment

- foil
- tongs
- chopping board
- medium frying pan
- spatula or wooden spoon
- jug
- whisk or fork
- small sharp knife

frying pan

spatula

1 Preheat the grill to medium-high. Line the grill pan with foil and grill the sausages all over for 10-15 mins, or until cooked through and golden brown.

2 While the sausages are cooling slightly, cut the cooked potatoes into bite-sized chunks. Then cut the cooled sausages into 2.5cm (1in) pieces.

Food Facts

The best sausages are called 'lean' and contain much less fat and fewer additives than poor quality sausages. Turkey sausages usually have a lower fat content than those made from red meats such as pork or beef.

sausages

Tasty Twists

Vegetarian sausages, lean bacon or cooked chicken would also taste great in this tortilla. Other vegetables such as mushrooms, peppers or asparagus could also be added.

3 Heat the oil in a frying pan. Add the potatoes and fry them over a medium heat for 8 minutes or until golden. Add the tomatoes and cook for 2 mins.

4 Crack the eggs into a jug and then beat them together. Season the beaten eggs with salt and pepper. Add the sausages to the frying pan.

5 Add a little more oil to the frying pan if necessary. Pour the eggs into the pan and cook, without stirring, for 5 minutes until the base of the tortilla is set.

6 To cook the top of the tortilla, carefully place the pan under the grill and cook for another 3–5 minutes, or until the top is set.

7 Carefully remove the pan from the grill and leave to cool slightly before sliding the tortilla on to a serving plate. Cut into wedges and serve.

Light Meals

It is important to keep energy levels up throughout the day. Regular meals are essential, but topping them up with a couple of healthy snacks will help to give concentration and memory a boost. There are plenty of recipes for delicious and nutritious light meals and snacks to choose from in this section, but here are some more to try!

Veggie Burgers

Put 125g (4½oz) tinned kidney beans (drained), 1 small onion (chopped), 1 carrot, 50g (2oz) wholemeal breadcrumbs, 1 tablespoon peanut butter (optional) and 1 egg into a food processor. Process to a coarse purée, season and chill the mixture for 1 hour. Form into 4 burgers and dust each one in flour. Brush with oil and grill for 5–6 minutes on each side.

Crudités

Most vegetables are better for you when they are raw. Try dipping strips of raw vegetables such as celery, peppers, carrots or cucumber into houmous or guacamole.

Houmous

Blend 400g (14oz) tinned chickpeas (drained), 2 garlic cloves (peeled), 2 tbsp sesame seed paste (tahini), the juice of 1 lemon and 4 tbsp olive oil, until smooth and creamy.

Toast Toppings

Mash ½ ripe avocado then spread it thickly on top of wholemeal toast. Houmous or peanut butter taste great on toast too!

Simply Souper!

Boost the nutritional content of shop-bought soups by adding tinned beans, cooked lentils or extra vegetables.

Coleslaw

Add ½ finely shredded small white or red cabbage, 2 grated carrots, 1 grated apple and 2 chopped spring onions to a bowl. Mix together 2 tbsp olive oil, 1 tbsp lemon juice and 4 tbsp mayonnaise and stir into the cabbage mixture.

Burger Relish

Roughly chop 4 tomatoes, 1 large apple (peeled and cored) and 1 onion. Place them in a saucepan with 75ml (3fl oz) white wine vinegar and 50g (2oz) sugar. Bring to the boil, then reduce the heat, cover, and simmer for 15 minutes. Uncover the pan and cook for another 20 minutes, or until soft. Purée if you prefer a smooth relish.

Nut Butter

Place 75g (3oz) shelled nuts, such as peanuts, cashews or hazelnuts, in a dry frying pan. Toast them for 2–3 minutes over a medium-low heat, until light golden. (Stir frequently to prevent burning.) Put the nuts in a food processor and process until finely chopped. Pour in 3–4 tablespoons sunflower oil and process to a coarse paste. Store in an airtight jar.

Miso Soup

Miso is made from fermented soya beans and is usually bought in dried or paste form. For a more filling soup, add water plus cooked egg noodles and thin slices of spring onion, carrot and red pepper.

Jacket Potato

Preheat an oven to 200°C (400°F/ Gas 6). Scrub the potatoes and prick with a fork or insert a skewer through the middle. Bake for 1–1½ hours, until tender in the centre and the skin is crisp. Serve with a healthy filling such as tuna, sweetcorn and peppers.

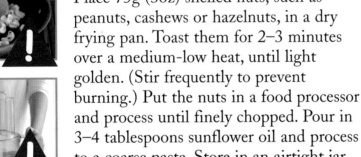

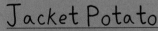

Corn Chowder

This recipe will really warm you up on a cold day! Chowder is a special kind of thick soup from New England in the USA. Although some chowders include fish, this simple recipe relies on nutritious potatoes, sweetcorn and carrot. It tastes great served with the rolls from p.122–123.

Helpful Hint

If you prefer a chunky soup, leave out step 5. For a smooth soup, blend all the mixture in step 5 until it is creamy.

Ingredients

potatoes

- 1 large onion
- 200g (9oz) fresh, frozen or tinned sweetcorn
- 1 large carrot
- 350g (12oz) potatoes
- 1 tbsp sunflower oil
- 1 bouquet garni (optional)
- 1 bay leaf
- 1.2 litres (2 pints) vegetable stock
- 300ml (10fl oz) milk
- salt and pepper

onion

carrot

Equipment

vegetable peeler

- small sharp knife
- vegetable peeler
- chopping board
- large saucepan with lid
- wooden spoon
- blender

wooden spoon

1 Peel and roughly chop the onion. Scrub the carrot and then thinly slice it. Finally, peel the potatoes and then cut them into small pieces.

2 Heat the oil in a saucepan. Add the onion and sauté over a medium heat for 8 minutes or until soft and slightly golden. Stir the onion occasionally.

3 Next, add the corn, carrot, potatoes, bouquet garni and bay leaf to the onions. Cook for 2 minutes, stirring constantly. Add the stock and bring to the boil.

Season your soup to taste with the salt and pepper.

Tasty Twists

Chunks of smoked haddock would add a delicious smoky flavour to this soup. Add the fish in step 4 with the milk and simmer for 5 minutes or until cooked.

Food Facts

Rich in complex carbohydrates, sweetcorn is also a good source of vitamins A, B and C. If you use tinned sweetcorn instead of fresh, make sure you buy the type without added salt or sugar.

sweetcorn

4 Reduce the heat to medium to low. Cover with a lid and cook for 15 minutes, stirring occasionally. Add the milk and cook for a further 5 minutes.

5 Scoop out some of the vegetables and blend the rest of the soup until smooth. Return the vegetables and blended soup to the pan and warm through.

Picnic Salad

This recipe is a simplified version of a traditional Greek salad. You could substitute the feta with any of your favourite cheeses such as Cheddar, mozzarella or brie and add other ingredients, such as olives, peppers, spring onions and lettuce.

Tasty Twists
Tinned beans such as chickpeas, cannellini or borlotti beans are a great alternative to cheese. Tuna, salmon or prawns would also taste delicious.

Ingredients

pitta breads

- 2 wholemeal pitta breads
- 1 small cucumber
- 12 small tomatoes (quartered)
- ½ red onion (thinly sliced)
- 150g (5½ oz) feta cheese (cut into chunks)

Dressing:
- 3 tbsp olive oil
- 1 tbsp lemon juice or white wine vinegar
- ½ tsp Dijon mustard

onion

tomatoes

cucumber

Equipment

- small sharp knife
- chopping board
- teaspoon
- clean, empty jam jar
- mixing bowl

mixing bowl

sharp knife

1 Preheat the grill to medium. Cut along one side of each pitta to open it up. Toast the pitta breads on both sides until golden and crisp. Leave to cool.

2 Slice the cucumber in half lengthways and then scoop out the seeds using a teaspoon. Cut the lengths in half and then chop into bite-sized pieces.

3 Put the cucumber, tomatoes and red onion into a salad bowl. Cut the cooled pitta breads into small pieces and add them to the bowl.

This salad also tastes delicious with a sprinkling of chopped fresh mint.

4 To make the dressing, put the olive oil, lemon juice and mustard into a clean jar. Put the lid on and shake until the ingredients are mixed together.

5 Pour the dressing over the salad. Mix the salad using clean hands until it is coated in the dressing. Finally, scatter over the feta cheese and then serve.

Food Facts

True feta cheese is only produced in Greece. Traditionally it was made from ewes' milk but nowadays it is often made with cows' or goats' milk. Like all cheeses, feta is an excellent source of calcium and protein. However, it is also high in fat so it should be eaten in moderation.

feta cheese

- **Preparation** 15 mins • **Cooking** 12 mins • **Serves** 2–4

Baked Eggs and Ham

These pies are so simple to make and taste delicious. Traditional pastry is high in fat so this recipe uses ham as a base instead. Serve with ripe, juicy tomatoes or crunchy salad. They're perfect for brunch too.

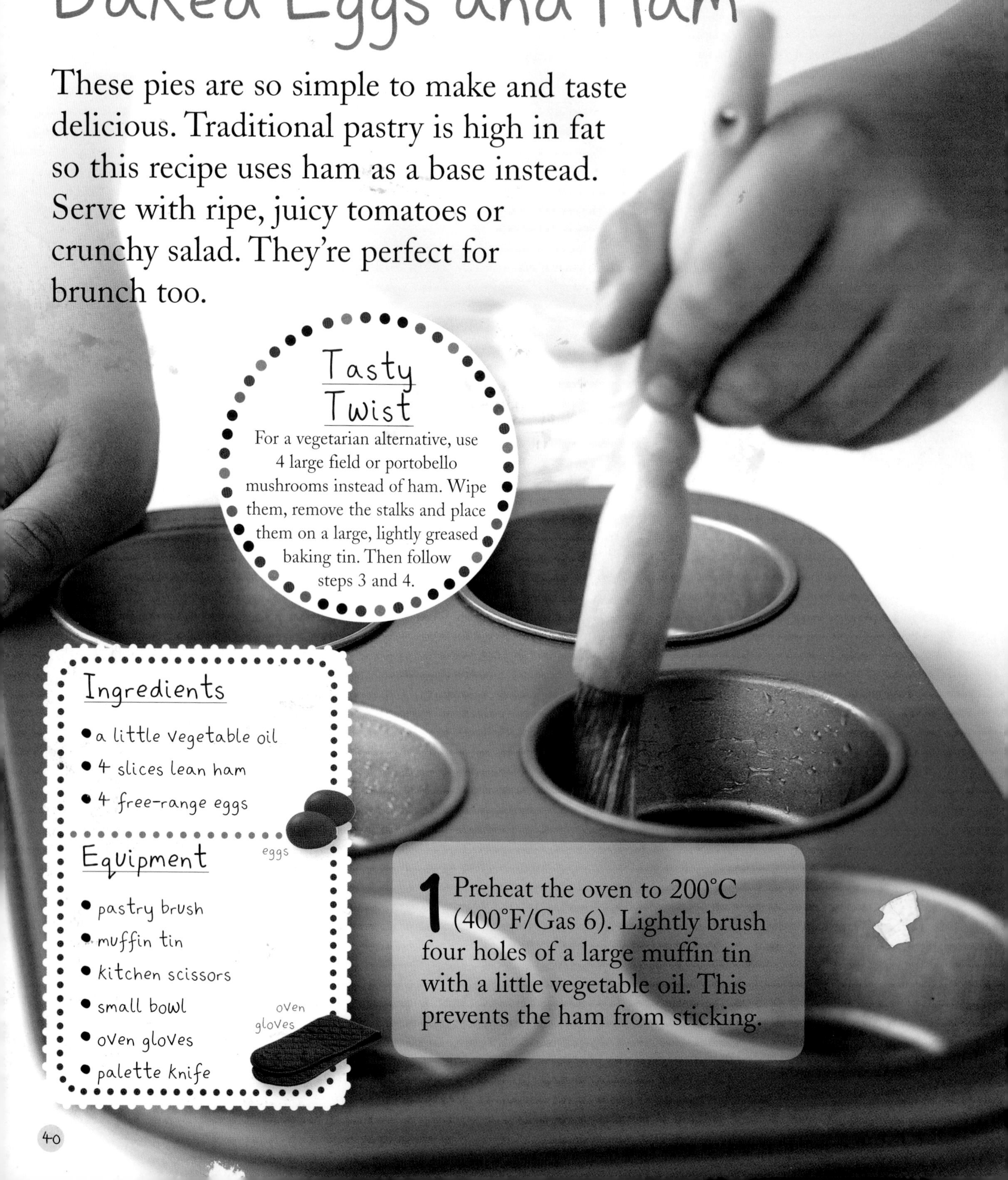

Tasty Twist

For a vegetarian alternative, use 4 large field or portobello mushrooms instead of ham. Wipe them, remove the stalks and place them on a large, lightly greased baking tin. Then follow steps 3 and 4.

Ingredients

- a little vegetable oil
- 4 slices lean ham
- 4 free-range eggs

eggs

Equipment

- pastry brush
- muffin tin
- kitchen scissors
- small bowl
- oven gloves
- palette knife

oven gloves

1 Preheat the oven to 200°C (400°F/Gas 6). Lightly brush four holes of a large muffin tin with a little vegetable oil. This prevents the ham from sticking.

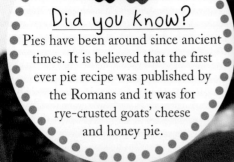

Did you know?

Pies have been around since ancient times. It is believed that the first ever pie recipe was published by the Romans and it was for rye-crusted goats' cheese and honey pie.

boiled egg

Food Facts

Eggs can be cooked in many different ways. In this recipe the eggs are baked in the oven until set but they can also be fried, boiled, scrambled or poached. To tell if an egg is fresh, place it in a bowl of water — if it sinks and lays flat it is fresh.

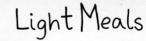

2 Arrange a slice of ham in each hole. Carefully trim the slices to make them even, but make sure that the ham is still slightly above the edge of the tin.

3 One by one, crack an egg into a small bowl and pour it into each ham-lined hollow. Bake in the oven for 10–12 minutes, or until the egg has set.

4 Using oven gloves, remove the tray from the oven and leave it to cool for a few minutes. Then carefully lift out the pies with a palette knife.

Tuna Quesadillas and Carrot Salad

Quesadillas are simple to prepare and taste great with a variety of interesting fillings. Best of all, they are delicious hot or cold.

Tasty Twists

For an equally colourful vegetarian alternative, try pesto, sliced tomato and mozzarella. You could also try the bean filling from p.60–61.

Ingredients

- 2 soft flour tortillas
- 60g (2½ oz) tinned tuna in spring water (drained)
- 40g (1½ oz) mature Cheddar (grated)
- 2 spring onions (peeled and sliced)

Cheddar cheese

- ½ small orange pepper (deseeded and cut into small pieces)
- a little olive oil

Carrot Salad

- 1 large carrot
- 2 tbsp raisins
- 1 tbsp pine nuts
- 1 tbsp olive oil
- 2 tsp lemon juice

spring onions

orange pepper

Equipment

- spoon
- chopping board
- frying pan
- spatula
- 2 dinner plates
- small sharp knife
- fork
- grater
- 2 mixing bowls

chopping board

frying pan

Food Facts

Tuna is an oily fish so it contains healthy omega-3 fats (although tinned tuna has less omega-3 than fresh, see p.58). Tuna also provides vitamins B, D and E.

tuna

1 Lay out one of the tortillas on a board or a clean and dry work surface. Leaving a 2cm (¾in) border around the edge, spoon the tuna over the top.

2 Sprinkle the Cheddar cheese over the tuna and then add the spring onions and orange pepper. Place the second tortilla on top and press down firmly.

3 Brush a large frying pan with olive oil. Cook the quesadilla for 2 minutes over a medium heat. Press down with a spatula to make sure the cheese melts.

4 Now you need to turn the quesadilla over. Carefully slide it onto a large plate. Put another plate on top and gently turn the plates over.

5 Carefully put the quesadilla back in the pan and cook the other side for 2 minutes. Remove the cooked quesadilla from the pan and cut it into wedges.

Did you know?
Carrots were first grown in Afghanistan in the 7th century. At that time they were red, black, yellow, white or purple, not orange.

1 Carefully grate the carrot and then put it into a mixing bowl. Add the raisins and pine nuts to the bowl and mix everything together.

2 To make the dressing, mix together the olive oil and lemon juice using a fork. Pour the mixture over the carrot salad and stir to coat the salad evenly.

Colourful Seafood Salad

Protein, carbohydrates, vitamins, minerals, healthy fats – this salad has it all! In the green corner, avocadoes contain more protein than any other fruit and are also rich in beta carotene and vitamin E. While in the red corner, tomatoes are good for your immune system and an excellent source of vitamins A, C and E.

Healthy Hints
If you don't like prawns or can't get hold of them, cooked chicken is a healthy alternative. Vegetarians could add cooked tofu or pine nuts instead.

Ingredients

- 150g (5½ oz) pasta shells
- 250g (9oz) cooked peeled prawns
- 12 small tomatoes (quartered)
- 1 large avocado
- lettuce leaves (cut into strips)

Dressing:
- 4 tbsp mayonnaise
- 2 tsp lemon juice
- 2 tbsp tomato ketchup
- 2 drops Tabasco sauce (optional)
- salt and pepper

avocadoes

tomatoes

pasta shells

Equipment

- large saucepan
- wooden spoon
- small sharp knife
- chopping board
- mixing bowl
- small bowl
- teaspoon

mixing bowl

chopping board

1 Bring a large saucepan of water to the boil. Add the pasta and follow the cooking instructions on the packet. Drain well and leave to cool.

2 Carefully cut the avocado around its middle and gently prise it apart. Scoop out the stone with a teaspoon and then cut each half into quarters.

3 Peel off the skin and cut the avocado into chunks. Put the avocado into a bowl and spoon over half of the lemon juice to stop the fruit turning brown.

Although avocadoes are high in fat, it is the good monounsaturated kind.

Did you know?
Avocadoes were first cultivated in South America. It was believed that a Mayan princess ate the very first avocado and that it held magical powers.

Food Facts

Like all shellfish, prawns are packed full of healthy minerals and are bursting with flavour. Prawns help to boost the immune system because they contain important minerals called zinc and selenium.

prawns

4 Put the tomatoes, avocado and prawns into a bowl with the pasta and season. Divide the shredded lettuce leaves between the serving bowls.

5 Mix together all the ingredients for the dressing in a small bowl. Add the pasta salad to the serving bowls and then drizzle over the dressing.

Italian Pasta Soup

This wholesome, tasty soup is based on a traditional Italian soup called minestrone. With the pasta, vegetables and Parmesan topping it is a complete meal in a bowl!

Minestrone was originally eaten by poor Italians and was made with whatever ingredients were available.

Tasty Twists

Meat eaters could add some bacon to the soup, but make sure you cook it thoroughly in step 3. Tinned mixed beans, green beans, courgettes or peppers would also taste great.

Ingredients

potatoes

- 75g (3oz) pasta bows
- 1 large onion
- 2 potatoes
- 2 sticks celery
- 1 large carrot (scrubbed)
- 1 tbsp olive oil
- 1 bay leaf
- 1 tsp dried oregano
- 1 litre (1¾ pints) vegetable stock
- 400g (14oz) tinned chopped tomatoes
- Parmesan cheese (grated)

pasta bows

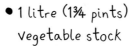 carrot

Equipment

- small sharp knife
- chopping board
- medium saucepan
- wooden spoon
- large saucepan with lid
- ladle

ladle

saucepan

1 Bring a medium-sized pan of water to the boil and add the pasta. Simmer until the pasta is just tender but not completely cooked. Drain well and set aside.

2 Chop the onion into small pieces. Peel the potatoes and cut them into bite-sized chunks. Slice the celery and carrot into bite-sized pieces.

Did you know?
Many people think that Venetian explorer Marco Polo introduced pasta to Italy from China in the 13th century. In fact, pasta has been eaten in Italy since as far back as Roman times!

Helpful Hint
When you drain the pasta in step 1, rinse it with cold water to prevent it sticking together and cooking further.

3 Heat the olive oil in a large saucepan. Add the onion and fry over a medium heat for 8 minutes or until it is softened and golden.

4 Next, add the celery, carrot, potatoes, oregano and bay leaf. Stir well and pour in the stock and chopped tomatoes. Stir again and then bring to the boil.

5 When the soup is bubbling, reduce the heat to low. Half-cover the pan with a lid and simmer the soup for 15 minutes or until the potatoes are tender.

6 Remove the lid, add the pasta and stir well. Heat the pasta for 5 minutes. Ladle the soup into large bowls and sprinkle with Parmesan cheese.

Food Facts

Pasta is a carbohydrate food and it gives the body energy. Surprisingly it also provides a small amount of protein. It is best to use wholewheat pasta because it is higher in fibre, vitamins and minerals than white pasta.

wholewheat pasta

Pitta Pockets

Tofu is a very versatile and nutritious ingredient. It naturally has a mild flavour but when marinated it takes on the flavour of the marinade. The sauce used in this recipe gives the tofu a delicious barbecue taste as well an appetising golden glow.

Did you know?
Tofu is also known as bean curd. Soya beans are cooked, puréed and drained to produce a milky liquid. The liquid is mixed with a coagulant to form a custard or cheese-like substance.

Ingredients

- 250g (9oz) firm tofu
- a little olive oil
- 3 Cos lettuce leaves (shredded)
- 2 spring onions (peeled and cut into long strips)
- a handful of alfalfa sprouts (optional)

tofu   *pitta breads*

- 4 wholemeal pitta breads (warmed in a toaster or warm oven)

Marinade
- 2 tbsp sweet chilli sauce
- 2 tbsp tomato ketchup
- 2 tbsp soy sauce
- ½ tsp ground cumin

Equipment

- small sharp knife
- chopping board
- kitchen towel
- dessertspoon
- shallow dish
- griddle pan
- spatula or tongs

griddle pan

tongs

1 In a shallow dish, mix together all the ingredients for the marinade. Pat the tofu dry with a kitchen towel and then cut it into 8 long slices.

2 Put the tofu into the dish with the marinade. Spoon the marinade over the tofu until it is well coated. Leave the tofu to marinate for at least 1 hour.

3 Brush the griddle pan with a generous amount of olive oil and then put it on the heat. Carefully put 4 of the tofu slices into the hot pan.

You could use the marinades from p.74–75 and p.78–79.

Tasty Twists

Strips of chicken, pork, turkey or beef or even a medley of vegetables such as pepper, courgette and onion make a great alternative to the tofu.

4 Cook the tofu for 4 minutes on each side, or until golden. As you cook, spoon over more of the marinade. Cook the remaining 4 slices of tofu in the same way.

5 Carefully slice along the edge of the pitta breads. Divide the lettuce, spring onions and alfalfa sprouts between the pitta breads and then add 2 pieces of tofu.

Food Facts

Alfalfa is a seed with a long, slender shoot and a clover-like leaf that is usually bought as a sprouted plant. It is one of the few plant foods that is a complete protein and it is also an excellent source of vitamins B and C.

alfalfa

Griddle Cakes

These American-style savoury pancakes are perfect for a light but filling meal or as a tasty weekend brunch.

Helpful Hints
Keep the bacon and cooked pancakes warm in the oven while you cook the rest of the griddle cakes. They are delicious served with guacamole.

Did you know?
Corn is a member of the grass family so it isn't really a vegetable, it's a grain. The average ear of sweetcorn has 800 kernels, arranged in 16 rows.

Ingredients

wholemeal flour

- 110g (4oz) plain flour white or wholemeal
- 1 tsp bicarbonate of soda
- 1 tsp baking powder
- 1 free-range egg
- 100ml (3½ fl oz) milk
- 75g (3oz) sweetcorn (fresh, frozen or tinned)

- 284ml (10fl oz) carton buttermilk
- 3 tsp sunflower oil
- 8 lean bacon rashers
- salt and pepper

sweetcorn

bacon

Equipment

- small jug
- fork or whisk
- sieve
- large mixing bowl
- wooden spoon
- tin foil
- large frying pan
- ladle
- spatula

whisk

frying pan

1 Pour the milk into a jug and then carefully crack the egg straight into the jug. Mix the milk and egg together with a fork or small whisk.

2 Sieve the flour, bicarbonate of soda, baking powder and a pinch of salt into a large mixing bowl. Make a well in the centre of the bowl.

3 Pour the milk and egg mixture into the well in the centre of the flour mixture. Then carefully add the buttermilk and sweetcorn.

4 Gently beat the mixture until the ingredients are combined. Cover the mixture with a plate and leave to stand while you cook the bacon.

5 Line the grill rack with foil and preheat the grill to medium. Put the bacon under the grill and cook for 2-3 minutes on each side, or until crisp.

6 Heat half the oil in the pan and then ladle in the batter to make griddle cakes about 10cm (4in) in diameter. Make sure there is space between the cakes.

7 Cook for 2-3 minutes, until golden underneath. Flip and then cook the other side. Make 12 cakes in this way, adding the rest of the oil when necessary.

Food Facts

Like all dairy foods, milk is an excellent source of calcium and phosphorus, both of which are essential for healthy teeth and bones. Interestingly, there's exactly the same amount of calcium in skimmed milk as there is in whole milk. Zinc and B vitamins are also provided by milk along with antibodies which help boost the immune system and the digestive system.

milk

Pizzettas

Traditionally, a pizza base is made using yeast which helps it to rise. These yeast-free pizzettas are made with a base that does not need time-consuming kneading or rising but still tastes light and crisp.

Tasty Twists

You can add any of your favourite toppings in step 7 before sprinkling the Cheddar. Mushrooms, peppers, onions, rocket, tuna, prawns, ham, olives, pepperoni and cooked chicken all taste great!

Ingredients

wholemeal flour

- 275g (9½ oz) white or wholemeal self-raising flour (plus extra for dusting)
- ½ tsp salt
- 125–150ml (4–5fl oz) semi-skimmed milk
- 4 tbsp olive oil

mozzarella

Topping:
- 1 quantity Tomato Dipping Sauce (see page 68–69)
- 150g (5½ oz) ball mozzarella (drained)
- 50g (2oz) mature Cheddar (grated)

Equipment

- sieve
- large mixing bowl
- wooden spoon
- rolling pin
- 2 large baking sheets
- spoon

sieve

mixing bowl

rolling pin

1 Preheat the oven to 200°C (400°F/Gas 6). Sieve the flour and salt into a mixing bowl and then make a well in the centre of the mixture.

2 Pour the milk and oil into the well. Mix with a wooden spoon until the flour and liquids start to come together and form a soft dough.

3 Lightly dust a work top and your hands with flour. Tip the dough out of the bowl and knead it for about 1 minute to form a smooth ball.

4 Dust 2 baking sheets with flour. Divide the dough into 4 smaller balls. Using a rolling pin, roll each piece into a 15cm (6in) circle.

Food Facts
Cheese provides valuable amounts of protein and calcium. However, cheese, especially hard cheese like Cheddar, is high in saturated fat so try to eat moderate amounts. Choose a mature cheese as its strong flavour means that you need less.

Cheddar cheese

5 Carefully place 2 dough bases on each baking sheet. Top each base with 1–2 tablespoons of the Tomato Dipping Sauce (see p.68–69).

6 Using the back of a spoon, spread the tomato in an even layer almost to the edge of the pizza base. Slice the mozzarella ball into 8–12 pieces.

7 Add the mozzarella and any other toppings. Top with the Cheddar cheese. Bake the pizzas for 10 mins or until the base has risen and the top is golden.

Homemade Burgers

This tasty, low-fat turkey burger is a healthy winner when partnered with a high-fibre bun. It's sure to get gobbled up in no time!

Tasty Twists

Vegetarians could use the Veggie Burgers recipe on p. 34, and meat eaters could try pork, beef or lamb mince as a tasty alternative

See p.35 for the Burger Relish recipe.

Ingredients

- 1 small onion
- 1 apple
- 450g (1lb) lean turkey, chicken, beef, pork or lamb mince
- 1 small egg
- plain flour
- salt and pepper

apples

wholemeal flour

burger buns

To serve

- seeded burger buns (preferably wholemeal)
- lettuce leaves
- sliced tomatoes
- relish (see p.   35)

lettuce leaves

Equipment

- grater
- mixing bowl
- wooden spoon
- small bowl
- fork or whisk
- cling film
- large plate
- tin foil
- tongs

wooden spoon

mixing bowl

1 Peel and then finely chop the onion. Leaving the skin on, coarsely grate the apple. When you can see the core and pips – it's done!

2 Put the onion and apple into a mixing bowl and add the mince. Stir or use your hands to break up the mince and mix it with the onion and apple.

3 Crack an egg into a separate bowl and lightly beat the yolk and white together, using a fork or whisk. This will help bind the burger mixture together.

4 Pour the beaten egg into the mince, onion and apple mixture. Season, then using clean hands mix it all together – this part is messy but a lot of fun!

5 Lightly cover a plate and your hands with flour. Take a handful of the mixture and shape into a round, flat burger. Put it onto the floured plate.

6 Do the same with the rest of the mixture and then lightly dust all 6 burgers with flour. Cover with cling film and chill for at least 30 minutes.

Food Facts

Turkey is a versatile meat that contains an array of valuable nutrients, including iron, zinc and selenium. It is a good source of B vitamins, which are essential for the body's processing of foods. Turkey is also high in protein and low in fat, making it one of the healthiest meats of all.

turkey mince

7 Preheat the grill to medium. Place the burgers onto a foil-covered grill rack and cook them for 8 minutes on each side, or until cooked through.

Main Meals

Easy Pizza

Make shop-bought pizza healthier by adding your favourite toppings. Sweetcorn, mushrooms, olives, peppers or spinach add essential vitamins and minerals while ham, egg, tuna or prawns are good sources of protein.

Pasta Salad

Salads can be much more than a side dish. Cook 125g (4½oz) pasta according to the packet instructions and then stir in 4 tbsp pesto (see p.64–65). Cut a 150g (5½oz) ball of mozzarella into bite-sized pieces and stir into the pasta. Add a handful of basil leaves and 12 halved cherry tomatoes. Finish off with a sprinkling of pine nuts.

Balance is the key to a healthy main meal, so imagine that your plate is divided into three parts. A carbohydrate food such as pasta, potatoes or rice should form the main part of your meal; there should also be a protein food such as meat, fish, poultry, eggs, nuts or pulses and finally, some vegetables. Eat at least 2 hours before going to bed to give your body time to digest your food properly. You'll find lots of great recipe ideas in this section, but here are some simple ideas to tempt your tastebuds.

Sausage and Veg Roast

Preheat the oven to 200°C (400°F/Gas 6). Place chunks of butternut squash, potato, wedges of onion and some sausages in a roasting tin with 1 tbsp olive oil. Roast in the oven for 20 minutes. Remove from the oven, turn the vegetables and sausages so they brown evenly then add some cherry tomatoes. Return to the oven for another 10–15 minutes.

Steamed Veg

Steamed vegetables are cooked over water, not in water, as they are when boiled. This preserves many of the vitamins, especially the water-soluble ones.

Couscous

Couscous is a tasty alternative to rice or pasta. Put 225g (8oz) couscous into a bowl and pour in enough boiling water or stock to just cover the couscous. Stir the couscous with a fork and leave to stand for 5–10 minutes, or until the liquid has been absorbed. Fluff up the couscous with a fork before serving.

Baked Beans

For homemade baked beans, combine 200g/7oz tinned haricot beans (drained and rinsed), 150ml (5fl oz) passata, 1 tsp Dijon mustard and 1 tbsp each of olive oil, Worcestershire sauce, maple syrup and tomato purée in a saucepan. Bring to the boil then reduce the heat. Half-cover the pan and simmer for 15–20 minutes until the sauce has thickened, stirring occasionally.

Nuts and Seeds

Sprinkle a handful of nuts and seeds over salads, stir-fries, noodles or rice. Just a handful can boost levels of vitamins B and E, iron, zinc and omega-6 essential fats. Walnuts and pumpkin seeds also contain omega-3 fats.

Stir Fry

Stir-frying is a healthy and quick way of cooking. Cut the ingredients into similar size pieces so they cook equally and use a small amount of oil. Carrots, peppers, mangetout, courgettes, mushrooms, onions and beansprouts all taste great stir-fried.

Mashed Potato

For tasty and colourful mash, try adding carrots, celeriac, squash, swede or sweet potato. Use equal amounts of potato and the vegetable of your choice and cook in boiling water for 15–20 minutes, or until tender. Drain, then return to the pan and mash. Add milk and a little butter to make a creamy mash.

Tuna Pasta

Tuna is a good source of low-fat protein and a very common addition to pasta in Italy. Although tinned tuna is slightly lower in omega-3 fat than fresh, it still provides valuable brain-boosting nutrients. Best if all, this simple dish takes only minutes to make!

Tasty Twists

Serve with a green vegetable. Steamed broccoli is a great choice – the vitamin C in the tomato sauce will help your body absorb the iron in the broccoli. To give the sauce a protein boost, add some canned beans, such as chickpeas.

Ingredients

- 275g (9½ oz) pasta bows
- 2 tbsp olive oil
- 2 large cloves garlic (crushed)
- 1 tsp dried oregano (optional)
- 2 tsp tomato purée
- 800g (1lb 5oz) tinned chopped tomatoes
- ½ tsp sugar (optional)
- 200g (7oz) tinned tuna in olive oil (drained and broken up into chunks)
- salt and pepper

garlic   *pasta bows*

Equipment

- small sharp knife
- chopping board
- medium saucepan with lid
- large saucepan
- wooden spoon
- colander
- tablespoon

colander

saucepan

1 Bring a large saucepan of water to the boil. Add the pasta and cook according to the packet instructions, until the pasta is tender but not too soft.

2 Meanwhile, heat the oil in a saucepan, over a medium heat. Fry the garlic for 1 minute. Stir in the oregano, the chopped tomatoes and tomato purée.

3 Bring the sauce to the boil and reduce the heat. Half cover the pan and simmer for 15 mins or until the sauce has reduced by a third and thickened.

You only need to add sugar in step 4 if the tomatoes taste a little sharp.

Food Facts

Tomatoes get their red colour from lycopene. It is one of the few nutrients that is more easily absorbed by the body when it is heated or in a concentrated form, such as in a purée or sauce. Great for strengthening our immune systems and fighting colds, lycopene is an important antioxidant.

tomatoes

4 Stir the tuna into the sauce. Half-cover the pan and heat through for 2 mins, stirring occasionally. Add some sugar to the sauce if necessary and season.

5 Drain the pasta but save 2 tablespoons of the water. Return the pasta to the saucepan. Add the water and stir in the sauce until the pasta is coated.

Mixed Bean Burritos

A burrito is a delicious Mexican dish consisting of a rolled up flour tortilla filled with meat or vegetables.

Guacamole is the perfect accompaniment.

Ingredients

- 1 tbsp olive oil
- 1 large onion (chopped)
- 400g (14oz) tin mixed beans (drained and rinsed)
- 1 tsp dried oregano
- 400g (14oz) tin chopped tomatoes
- 1 tbsp tomato purée
- 1 tsp ground cumin
- few drops Tabasco (optional)
- salt and pepper

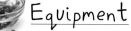
Cheddar cheese

To serve
- 4 soft flour tortillas
- 50g (2oz) mature Cheddar cheese (grated)
- shop-bought guacamole (optional)

Equipment

- small sharp knife
- chopping board
- medium saucepan with lid
- large spoon
- spatula or wooden spoon

chopping board

saucepan

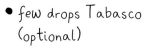
onion

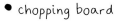
tortillas

1 Heat the oil in a medium-sized saucepan. Add the onion and cook, stirring occasionally, for 8 minutes until it is softened and slightly golden.

2 Add the oregano, chopped tomatoes, tomato purée and cumin to the saucepan. Tip the beans into the pan, stir and bring to the boil.

Tasty Twists

For a meaty filling, swap the beans for 400g (14oz) minced beef. Follow step 1 and then fry the mince for 5 minutes in step 2. Continue with steps 3 to 6.

3 When bubbling, reduce the heat to low. Half cover with a lid and simmer for 10 minutes. Stir the beans occasionally to stop them sticking.

4 Taste the beans and add salt and pepper along with a few drops of Tabasco if you like. Cook for another 5 minutes, stirring occasionally.

Food Facts

Beans are also known as pulses. They are an excellent combination of carbohydrates and protein and what's more they are low in fat. Beans also count as a portion in the five-a-day fruit and veg guidelines (see page 8–9).

mixed beans

Did you know?

The word burrito means 'little donkey' in Spanish. It is thought that the dish gets its name because a rolled up tortilla resembles the ear of a donkey!

5 Warm the tortilla in a microwave. Place each one on a plate and top with the bean stew. Sprinkle with Cheddar and top with a dollop of guacamole.

6 Fold in one end of the tortilla and then carefully fold over one side. Gently roll the tortilla over to make a tight and secure burrito.

Chicken Drumsticks

The yoghurt marinade gives the chicken drumsticks a lightly spiced flavour but also keeps them tender and tasty. All you need is a simple green salad and warm naan bread to serve.

These would also taste great cooked on a barbecue!

Ingredients

lemon

- 4 skinless chicken drumsticks

Marinade
- juice of ½ lemon
- 100ml (3½ fl oz) thick natural yoghurt

- 2 tbsp tandoori spice blend
- 1 tbsp sunflower oil

To serve
- mango chutney (optional)
- 4 small naan bread
- lettuce

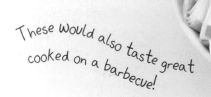

lettuce

naan bread

Equipment

- kitchen paper
- spoon
- large, shallow dish
- bowl
- cling film
- baking tray
- pastry brush
- tongs
- oven gloves

oven gloves

1 Pat the chicken with kitchen paper. Make three deep cuts in each drumstick and place them in a large, shallow dish. Squeeze the lemon juice over the drumsticks.

2 Put the yoghurt and tandoori spices in a bowl then mix together. Spoon the yoghurt marinade over the chicken until it is completely covered.

Tasty Twists

If you prefer meat without bones, choose chicken breasts instead of drumsticks. Follow steps 1–4 in the recipe and then cook the breasts for 20–25 minutes or until cooked through.

Did you know?

Spices are the seeds, fruit, pod, bark and buds of plants. They were once so prized that wars were fought over them, and they have even been used as currency in some countries.

3 Cover the drumsticks with cling film and chill them for at least 1 hour to marinate. After 50 minutes, preheat the oven to 200°C (400°F/Gas 6).

4 Brush the oil over the bottom of a baking tray. Place the chicken drumsticks on the baking tray and cook them in the oven for 15 minutes.

5 After 15 minutes, turn the chicken over and spoon over any remaining marinade. Cook the drumsticks for a further 15 minutes or until cooked through.

6 Check that the chicken is cooked through. (There should be no trace of pinkness.) Try serving with mango chutney, warm naan bread and lettuce.

Food Facts

Chicken is a great source of protein. It contains selenium, a nutrient that helps to fight infections. It is also low in fat, particularly if the skin is removed.

chicken

Pesto Pasta

Pasta is the ultimate quick, simple and nutritious meal. Try stirring in a spoonful of homemade pesto for an equally quick and mouthwateringly tasty sauce.

Tasty Twists

Peas, green beans, carrots or cauliflower could be used instead of the broccoli. Meat eaters could add some cooked chicken or bacon.

You could swirl a spoonful of pesto in soup, stir it into bread dough or spread it over toast.

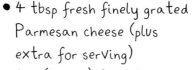

Ingredients

- 250g (9oz) spaghetti
- 15–20 small florets broccoli

spaghetti *salt* *pepper* *pine nuts*

Pesto

- 2 large cloves garlic (roughly chopped)
- 3 tbsp pine nuts

garlic

- 4 tbsp fresh finely grated Parmesan cheese (plus extra for serving)
- 60g (2½ oz) fresh basil leaves
- 75ml (3fl oz) olive oil
- salt and pepper

basil leaves

Equipment

- small sharp knife
- chopping board
- food processor
- jar with a lid
- large saucepan
- wooden spoon
- colander
- pasta spoon

colander *chopping board*

1 Put the garlic and pine nuts in a food processor and blend until coarsely chopped. Next, add the Parmesan and basil and blend again until a coarse purée.

2 Pour the olive oil into the food processor and blend to make a smooth mixture. Season to taste. Transfer the pesto to a jar with a lid.

Did you know?

Pesto is an Italian sauce from the city of Genoa that dates back to Roman times. The word 'pesto' comes from an Italian word meaning 'to crush'.

3 Fill a large saucepan three-quarters full of water. Add 1 teaspoon of salt and bring the water to the boil. Lower the pasta into the pan.

4 Cook the pasta according to the instructions on the packet. About 4 minutes before the pasta is cooked, add the broccoli and simmer.

5 Drain the pasta and broccoli but reserve 2 tablespoons of the cooking water. Return the pasta and broccoli to the pan with the cooking water.

Food Facts

Broccoli is a super-veg thanks to its impressive range of nutrients, from B vitamins and iron, to zinc and potassium. Broccoli belongs to the same family as cabbage, cauliflower, kale and brussel sprouts.

broccoli

6 Add enough pesto to coat the pasta and broccoli (you may have a some leftover). Stir and divide the pasta between four shallow bowls.

Griddled Chicken and Potato Salad

This healthy dish is really easy to make, but bursting with colour and flavour!

Helpful Hints

To check that the chicken is thoroughly cooked, insert a skewer or the tip of a knife into the thickest part – there should be no sign of any pink. If the chicken is not completely done, cook it for another minute or two.

The chicken could also be served with a green salad or on a bed of rice.

Ingredients

- 4 skinless chicken breasts (each about 150g/5½ oz)

Marinade
- 2 tsp paprika
- 3 tbsp olive oil

Potato Salad
- 400g (14oz) baby new potatoes (cut in half if necessary)
- 2 spring onions (finely chopped)
- 8 cherry tomatoes (halved)
- 3 tbsp chopped fresh mint
- 2 tbsp olive oil
- 1 tbsp lemon juice

spring onions

cherry tomatoes

Equipment
- large shallow dish
- tablespoon ● cling film
- griddle pan
- tongs
- small sharp knife
- chopping board
- medium saucepan
- salad bowl

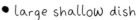
tongs

sharp knife

1 Mix the paprika and the olive oil in a large, shallow dish. Add the chicken and spoon over the marinade. Cover with cling film and chill for 30 minutes.

Food Facts

A griddle is similar to a frying pan but it is usually square and has a ridged base. This design makes griddling a healthier way of cooking because most of the fat collects in the ridges of the pan, rather than in the food itself. Meat, fish and vegetables can all be cooked on a griddle. As well as being a healthy way to cook, griddling also gives food a delicious, slightly barbecued flavour.

griddle

2 Heat a griddle pan until it is very hot. Reduce the heat to medium and place 2 chicken breasts in the pan. Griddle for 6 minutes on one side.

3 Carefully turn the chicken over using tongs. Spoon over a little of the marinade and then cook for another 6 minutes, or until cooked through.

4 Cook the remaining chicken breasts in the same way, making sure there is no trace of pink in the middle. Serve with the potato salad.

1 Put the potatoes in a medium saucepan and cover with water. Bring to the boil and cook the potatoes for 10 minutes or until they are tender.

2 Drain the potatoes and leave them to cool in a bowl. Finely chop the spring onions and halve the tomatoes. Put them in the bowl. Add the mint.

3 Mix the extra-virgin olive oil and lemon juice together, using a fork. Then pour the dressing over the salad and stir well to mix it in.

Lamb Kebabs and Tomato Dip

Soak the wooden skewers in water for 30 minutes to prevent them burning.

These kebabs contain just the right amount of spice to give them plenty of flavour without being too hot and spicy.

Did you know?
Many people believe that eating garlic prevents ageing. (It also keeps vampires away, of course!)

Ingredients

lean minced lamb

- 450g (1lb) lean minced lamb
- 1 small onion (finely chopped or processed)
- 2 cloves garlic (crushed)
- ½ tsp ground cinnamon
- 2 tsp ground cumin
- 1 tsp ground coriander
- olive oil (for brushing)
- salt and pepper

Tomato Dipping Sauce
- 2 tbsp olive oil
- 2 cloves garlic (crushed)
- 300ml (10fl oz) passata (sieved tinned tomatoes)
- 1 tbsp sun-dried tomato purée (or tomato purée)
- ½ tsp sugar

olive oil

Equipment
- medium saucepan
- large mixing bowl
- wooden spoon
- baking tray
- 12 wooden or metal skewers
- tongs

tongs

wooden skewer

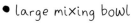

wooden spoon

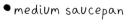

1 Pour the olive oil into a pan and heat gently. Fry the garlic for 1 minute, stirring constantly. Add the passata, tomato purée and sugar and bring to the boil.

2 Reduce the heat, partially cover the pan and simmer for 15 minutes. Stir the sauce occasionally to prevent it sticking to the bottom of the pan.

1 Put the lamb mince in a mixing bowl and break it up using a fork. Add the chopped onion, garlic, cinnamon, cumin and coriander to the bowl.

2 Season with salt and pepper and then stir the ingredients until they are all combined. Preheat the grill to medium and lightly oil a baking tray.

3 Divide the lamb mixture into 12 pieces. Shape each one into a sausage and then thread them onto the skewers. Press or roll to lengthen the kebabs.

4 Place the lamb kebabs onto the baking tray. Grill them for about 10 minutes. Turn them over halfway through, until golden all over and cooked through.

Food Facts

Every country in the world includes onions in its cooking and along with garlic, it has become an essential flavouring in a wide variety of dishes. For centuries, onions and garlic have also been used in all kinds of traditional remedies. Both are antibacterial and antiviral, helping to fight colds and relieve asthma and hayfever.

garlic

onion

Salmon Parcels

Salmon is full of brain-boosting, healthy oils that help with concentration and memory. If you are not usually a fan of fish, this tasty recipe might just win you over!

Did you know?
Japan consumes the highest amount of salmon per person, and has the lowest level of heart disease in the world.

Vegetarians could use a selection of vegetables such as carrot, red pepper, mangetout, broccoli, spring onions or courgettes.

Ingredients

- 2 tbsp sesame seeds
- 4 slices fresh ginger (peeled and cut into thin strips)
- 2 tbsp soy sauce
- 4 tbsp orange juice
- 4 thick salmon fillets (about 150g/5½ oz each)
- 1 carrot (cut into thin strips)
- 1 red pepper (deseeded and cut into thin strips)
- 3 spring onions (cut into thin strips)
- salt and black pepper
- 250g (9oz) noodles

carrot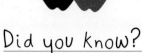

fresh ginger

noodles

Equipment

- small sharp knife
- chopping board
- frying pan
- baking tray
- baking parchment

sharp knife

chopping board

1 Preheat the oven to 200°C (400°F/Gas 6). Toast the sesame seeds in a dry frying pan until golden. Remove from the pan and set aside.

2 Cut the baking parchment into 4 pieces, at least twice the size of the salmon fillets. Place each piece of salmon on a piece of baking parchment.

3 Arrange a mixture of the carrot, red pepper, spring onion and ginger strips on top of each salmon fillet. Drizzle over the soy sauce and orange juice.

4 Season with salt and pepper. Carefully fold in the top and bottom of each parcel and then gather up the sides. Gently fold to make 4 loose parcels.

5 Put the parcels on a baking tray and bake for 15 minutes. Add the noodles to a pan of boiling water and cook, following the instructions on the packet.

Tasty Twists

Chicken breasts would also taste delicious cooked in this way. Follow the recipe but bake the chicken slightly longer than the salmon – about 20-25 minutes, or until cooked through.

6 Remove the fish from the oven and leave to cool slightly before opening the parcels. Serve with the noodles and a sprinkling of sesame seeds.

Food Facts

Salmon is an excellent source of polyunsaturated fatty acids, known as omega-3. These are the healthier kind of fats and have been shown to help reduce heart disease. They are good for the brain, skin, eyes and nerves too. (See p.14–15.)

salmon

Preparation 20 mins · **Cooking** 30 mins · **Serves** 4

Roasted Vegetable Pasta

Roasting vegetables is a great way to make them sweet and melt-in-your mouth tasty, without losing their goodness.

Tasty Twists

Butternut squash, aubergines, leeks or carrots would also taste great. Meat lovers could add ham or tinned tuna in step 2 or chicken, bacon or sausage that has been browned first.

Ingredients

- 1 aubergine
- 1 large courgette
- 1 large red onion
- 6 cloves garlic (whole)
- 1 large red pepper (deseeded)
- 3 tbsp olive oil
- 12 cherry tomatoes
- 300g (10½ oz) pasta spirals or tubes
- 4 tbsp low-fat crème fraiche
- 75g (3oz) mature Cheddar cheese (grated)
- 1 tbsp wholegrain mustard
- salt and pepper

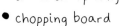
aubergine

Cheddar cheese

Equipment

- small sharp knife
- chopping board
- roasting tin
- large saucepan
- wooden spoon
- small mixing bowl
- teaspoon

saucepan

mixing bowl

72

1 Preheat the oven to 200°C (400°F/Gas 6). Slice the aubergine, courgette and red pepper into bite-sized chunks. Cut the onion into 8 wedges.

2 Put the aubergine, courgette, onion, garlic and red pepper in a roasting tin. Drizzle the oil over the vegetables and turn them so they are coated in it.

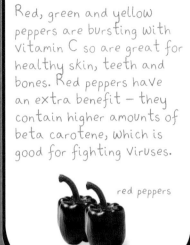

Food Facts

Red, green and yellow peppers are bursting with Vitamin C so are great for healthy skin, teeth and bones. Red peppers have an extra benefit – they contain higher amounts of beta carotene, which is good for fighting viruses.

red peppers

3 Roast for 15 minutes and then remove the tin from the oven. Add the tomatoes and coat them in the oil. Roast for 10 mins or until the vegetables are tender.

4 Meanwhile, bring a large saucepan of water to the boil. Add the pasta and cook according to the packet, until it is tender but not too soft.

Helpful Hint

There are lots of different pasta shapes to choose from. Opt for one that can 'hold' the sauce like penne, rigatoni or farfalle, rather than long pasta such as spaghetti or tagliatelle.

5 Remove the garlic cloves from the roasting tin. Drain the pasta and add it to the vegetables in the tin. Now peel and finely chop the garlic.

6 Mix the garlic with the crème fraîche and mustard. Add the crème fraîche mixture to the pasta and vegetables and sprinkle with the Cheddar.

7 Season and stir to mix it all together. Put the tin back in the oven for 5 minutes or until the cheese has melted and everything is warmed through.

Sticky Ribs with Baked Potato

The ribs can be marinated overnight for maximum flavour.

Give pork spare ribs a delicious sticky sweetness with this simple barbeque sauce – they're best eaten with your fingers!

Ingredients

- 1kg (2lb 4oz) pork spare ribs
- 4 medium baking potatoes (scrubbed)
- 4 tbsp sour cream (optional)
- 2 tbsp chopped chives (optional)

pork spare ribs

Marinade

- 2 tbsp honey
- 1 tbsp balsamic vinegar
- 4 tbsp tomato ketchup
- 2 tbsp soft brown sugar
- 1 tbsp Dijon mustard
- 1 tbsp olive oil
- 3 drops Tabasco (optional)

Tabasco

Equipment

- jug
- fork
- extra-wide foil
- baking tray
- oven gloves
- knife

baking tray

extra-wide foil

1 Put the marinade ingredients in a jug and mix them together. Place the ribs on a large piece of double-thickness foil. Pour the marinade over the ribs.

2 Make sure that the ribs are well coated. Scrunch the foil loosely around the ribs and twist to seal. Leave to marinate in the fridge for at least 1 hour.

3 Preheat the oven to 200°C (400°F/Gas 6). Scrub the potatoes and prick them all over with a fork. Bake the potatoes for 1 hour or until soft in the centre.

4 Remove the foil parcel with the ribs from the fridge and carefully place it onto a baking tray. Cook them in the oven with the potatoes for 30 minutes.

5 Carefully open up the foil parcel. Cook the ribs in the open parcel for a further 30 minutes, or until they are completely cooked.

Tasty Twists

This delicious marinade could be used to coat chicken, turkey, fish, vegetables and tofu. You could also try barbecuing instead of roasting.

6 Cut the potatoes in half and open them up. (Take care – they will be hot!) Top each potato with some sour cream and chives. Serve with the ribs.

Food Facts

Baking is a great way to cook potatoes. Not only is it a very simple method of cooking, but there is no need to add any fat. Potatoes are a popular starchy carbohydrate food and provide your body with energy as well as immunity-boosting vitamins B and C, plus iron and potassium. The skin contains the highest concentration of fibre, which helps your digestive system work efficiently.

potatoes

Jambalaya

This is a colourful Creole or Cajun rice dish from Louisiana in the USA. It is easy to make because all the ingredients are cooked in the same pot. The recipe can be adapted for vegetarians by swapping the chicken and ham for extra vegetables, meat-free sausages or tofu.

Tasty Twists

Prawns, pork, beans or vegetables, such as peas and courgettes, would also be tasty in this rice dish.

Ingredients

- 2 tbsp olive oil
- 3 skinless chicken breasts
- 1 large onion (chopped)
- 200g (7oz) smoked ham
- 2 large cloves garlic (chopped)
- 1 red pepper (deseeded and cut into bite-sized pieces)
- 1 tsp paprika
- 1 green chilli, deseeded and finely chopped (optional)
- 1 tsp dried thyme
- 700ml (1¼ pints) warm chicken or vegetable stock
- 3 tbsp tinned chopped tomatoes
- 250g (9oz) brown rice
- 50g (2oz) peas
- salt and pepper

pepper

peas

Equipment

- sieve
- small sharp knife
- chopping board
- large saucepan with lid
- wooden spoon

chopping board

saucepan

1 Put the rice in a sieve and rinse it under cold water until the water runs clear. Washing the rice before cooking stops the grains from sticking together.

2 Chop the onion into small pieces and set aside. Then carefully cut the chicken and ham into bite-sized pieces. Heat the oil in the large saucepan.

3 Fry the chicken and onion for 8 mins over a medium heat until the chicken is golden all over. Stir frequently to prevent the chicken sticking to the pan.

Add the peas 2 minutes before the rice is cooked in step 5 for extra colour and goodness!

Did you know?

One seed of rice yields more than 3,000 grains. It is the highest yielding cereal grain and can grow in many kinds of environments.

Food Facts

Rice is a staple food all over the world and its cultivation dates back to 5,000 BCE. It is an excellent source of energy. Brown rice is healthier than white rice because it contains fibre and richer amounts of vitamins and minerals. White rice has had the husk, bran and germ removed, which significantly reduces its nutritional value.

rice

4 Add the ham, garlic, red pepper and chilli, and cook for 2 mins. Add the paprika, thyme, rice, stock and tomatoes. Stir and bring to the boil.

5 Reduce the heat to low, cover the pan and simmer for 35 mins or until the rice is cooked and the stock is absorbed. Season the rice and stir before serving.

Colourful Kebabs

These are great fun to make and, of course, to eat! They would make a perfect vegetarian dish for a summer barbecue.

Tasty Twists

Cubes of chicken, beef, pork, lamb, or fish like salmon or tuna would all work in this recipe. Mushrooms, aubergine and spring onion could also be added to the red pepper, red onion and courgette.

Soak the wooden skewers in water for 30 minutes to prevent them burning.

Ingredients

- 250g (9oz) firm tofu
- 2 small courgettes (each cut into 8 pieces)
- 2 medium red onions (peeled and each cut into 8 wedges)
- 1 medium red pepper (deseeded and cut into 16 chunks)
- 250g (9oz) egg noodles
- 1 tbsp toasted sesame seeds (optional)

noodles

Marinade

- 2 tbsp olive oil
- 1 tbsp soy sauce
- 3 tbsp black bean sauce
- 1 tbsp clear runny honey
- 2 cloves garlic (crushed)
- salt and pepper

red onion

red pepper

Equipment

tongs

- large shallow dish
- large dish • kitchen towel
- sharp knife
- chopping board
- spoon
- 8 wooden or metal skewers
- pastry brush
- saucepan
- tongs and colander

colander

1 Pat the tofu dry with some kitchen paper and then cut it into 16 cubes. Put the cubes into the dish with the courgettes, onions and red pepper.

Tasty Twists

Swap the oriental marinade for a Mediterranean one. Mix together 4 tablespoons olive oil, 2 tablespoons balsamic vinegar, 2 crushed cloves garlic and 1 tablespoon clear runny honey.

Food Facts

Tofu is one of the few plant foods that is a complete protein. This means it contains a healthy balance of amino acids that are essential for repairing and maintaining your body. It is also low in fat and a good source of iron, calcium, magnesium and vitamins B1, B2, and B3. Firm tofu can be fried, stir-fried, deep-fried, sautéed or grilled. Because tofu itself is fairly bland, it is best marinated or used in recipes with strongly flavoured ingredients.

tofu

2 Mix the ingredients for the marinade in a large dish. Use a spoon to coat the tofu and vegetables in the marinade. Put in the fridge for at least 1 hour.

3 Preheat the grill to medium-high. Thread a piece of red pepper, tofu, red onion and courgette onto a skewer. Repeat and then make 7 more kebabs.

4 Place the kebabs on the grill and brush them with the marinade. Grill for 15–20 mins, turning halfway through and brushing with more marinade.

5 While the kebabs are cooking, bring a pan of water to the boil, add the noodles and cook as instructed on the packet. Drain the noodles in a colander.

6 Serve two kebabs per person. Arrange some noodles on a plate and place the kebabs on top. Sprinkle the sesame seeds over the noodles.

Sausage Hotpot

Fruit gives this savoury casserole a natural sweetness and an extra vitamin boost. Enjoy this winter warmer with fluffy mash and steamed green vegetables.

Tasty Twists
Turkey, pork, beef or vegetarian sausages would all work in this recipe. The sausages are browned in step 2 and then slowly cooked through in the oven.

See p.57 for a yummy Mashed Potato recipe idea.

Ingredients

- 2 eating apples
- 2 tbsp olive oil
- 6-8 sausages (turkey, pork, beef or vegetarian)
- 1 onion (chopped)
- 1 carrot (diced)
- 2 cloves garlic (finely chopped)
- 1 tsp mixed herbs
- 110g (4oz) lean bacon, cut into bite-sized pieces (optional)
- 400g (14oz) tinned borlotti or pinto beans (drained and rinsed)
- 400ml (14fl oz) chicken or vegetable stock
- 4 tbsp tinned chopped tomatoes
- 1 tbsp tomato purée
- salt and pepper

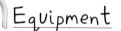

stock

sausages

Equipment

- vegetable peeler
- small sharp knife
- chopping board
- large ovenproof pan with lid (or large saucepan and large casserole dish with lid)
- oven gloves
- wooden spoon
- jug
- tongs

chopping board

saucepan

1 Carefully remove the skin of the apples using a vegetable peeler. Quarter them and remove the cores. Cut the apples into bite-sized pieces.

2 Preheat the oven to 200°C (400°F/Gas 6). Heat the oil in a large saucepan or ovenproof pan and cook the sausages for 5 minutes, or until browned all over.

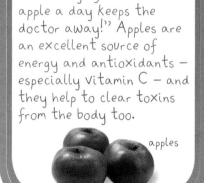

3 Remove the sausages from the pan and set aside. Put the onion and carrot into the pan and fry over a medium heat for 5 minutes, stirring frequently.

4 Next, add the garlic, bacon and herbs, stir well, and cook for 6 minutes. (Transfer to a large casserole dish if you aren't using an ovenproof pan.)

Did you know?
Sausages were called 'bangers' during the Second World War because they contained so much water they exploded when fried! Every day, 5 million Britons will eat sausages.

5 Add the beans, tomatoes, tomato purée, apples and sausages and stir. Pour in the stock and bring to the boil. Add the beans and stir well.

6 Cover with a lid and place in the preheated oven. Cook for 25 minutes. The sauce should reduce and thicken and the apples will become tender.

7 Take care when removing the casserole dish from the oven as the hotpot will be very hot. Season with salt and pepper. Serve with mash and vegetables.

Fish Sticks and Sweet Potato Wedges

Try this healthier version of traditional fish fingers and chips — it is easy to make and absolutely delicious!

Did you know?
Fish and chips shops first made an appearance in the UK at the end of the 19th century. Fish and chips quickly became Britain's most popular and famous fast food, and has remained so ever since.

Ingredients
- 400g (14oz) hoki fillets or other firm white fish (patted dry)
- 100g (3½ oz) fine cornmeal or polenta
- 2 tsp Cajun spice mix or paprika (optional)
- 1 free-range egg (beaten)
- salt and pepper
- 2 tbsp olive oil

Sweet Potato Wedges
- 2 large sweet potatoes (scrubbed)

polenta

fish fillets

Equipment
- small sharp knife
- chopping board
- kitchen towel
- roasting tin
- plate
- baking tray
- tongs

chopping board

baking tray

1 Preheat the oven to 200°C (400°F/Gas 6). Cut the sweet potatoes in half and then cut each half into smaller wedges. Pat the wedges dry with kitchen roll.

2 Put half of the oil into a roasting tin and add the potato wedges. Coat them in the oil and bake for 30 minutes, turning halfway through cooking.

Tasty Twist

You could also use ordinary baking potatoes instead of the sweet potatoes to make these crisp potato wedges. Just follow the recipe in exactly the same way.

3 Meanwhile, cut the hoki into 1cm (½in strips). Mix the cornmeal or polenta and the spices together on a plate. Season with salt and pepper.

4 One at a time, dip each fish strip into the beaten egg and then roll it in the cornmeal mixture until evenly coated. Repeat with all the fish sticks.

5 Add the remaining oil to a baking tray and then the fish sticks. When the wedges have been cooking for 22 minutes, put the fish sticks in the oven.

6 Bake the fish sticks for 8 minutes, turning halfway through. They should be golden and cooked through. Serve with the potato wedges and peas.

Food Facts

Choose the orange-fleshed sweet potatoes as they contain higher amounts of beta carotene than the white variety. Beta carotene is converted into vitamin A in your body.

sweet potatoes

Rainbow Beef

Stir-frying is a quick and easy way to make a colourful and nutritious meal. You could also serve this stir-fry with rice instead of noodles.

Did you know?
Mangetout means 'eat everything' in French, and they are so called because you eat the whole vegetable, including the pod. Mangetout are also called snow peas.

Ingredients

- 300 (10½ oz) lean beef (cut into thin strips)
- 1 tbsp sunflower oil
- 250g (9oz) medium egg noodles
- 1 red pepper (deseeded and cut into thin strips)
- 6 baby corn (halved)
- 75g (3oz) mangetout
- 3 spring onions (sliced on the diagonal)
- 2 cloves garlic (chopped)
- 2 tsp grated fresh ginger
- 4 tbsp fresh orange juice

Marinade
- 6 tbsp hoisin sauce
- 2 tbsp soy sauce
- 1 tbsp runny clear honey
- 1 tsp sesame oil

Equipment
- small sharp knife
- chopping board
- spoon
- shallow dish
- wok or large frying pan
- spatula or wooden spoon
- tongs
- medium saucepan
- colander

1 Put the marinade ingredients in a shallow dish. Mix them together and then add the beef strips. Coat them in the marinade, cover and set aside for 1 hour.

2 Heat the sunflower oil in a wok or frying pan. Remove the beef strips from the marinade using tongs and carefully put them into the wok or frying pan.

Food Facts

Stir-frying is a healthy method of preparing food because the ingredients are cooked quickly in a minimum amount of oil. This keeps the fat levels down and retains vital vitamins and minerals which are often destroyed by longer cooking times.

wok

3 Stirring continuously, fry the beef strips on a high heat for 1½ minutes or until browned all over. Remove the beef using the tongs and set aside.

4 Bring a saucepan of water to the boil. Add the noodles to the water, stir to separate them and then cook according to the packet instructions until tender.

Tasty Twists

Strips of pork and chicken are a good alternative to the beef, or you could try prawns or tofu. For the best flavour, it's important to marinate the meat first.

5 Add a little more oil to the wok if it looks dry. Add the red pepper, baby corn, mangetout and spring onions. Stir-fry for 2 minutes.

6 Add the garlic, ginger, beef and the leftover marinade and stir-fry for 1 minute. Pour in the orange juice, and cook, stirring, for another minute.

7 Drain the noodles in a colander and divide them between 4 shallow bowls. Spoon the vegetable and beef stir-fry over the noodles and serve.

Desserts

Being healthy doesn't mean you have to avoid desserts – a balanced diet means that you can eat most things, in moderation. In fact, dessert is an ideal opportunity to get more fruit into your diet! Just remember desserts and cakes can be high in fat, so eat sensibly. There's something for everyone in this section, from fruity jelly to crunchy crumble and from lovely lollies to apple muffins. Here are some more simple ideas for tasty desserts to try.

Fruit Purée
Simple fruit sauces are a tasty and nutritious accompaniment to yoghurt, ice cream and many other dishes. You need fruit with a soft, juicy texture such as mangoes, berries or nectarines. Purée your fruit in a blender, adding a little sugar if necessary.

Banana Custard
Mix together equal quantities of plain bio yoghurt and ready-made custard. Pile sliced bananas into a dish and pour over the yoghurt mixture. Stewed apples (see p.17) could be used instead.

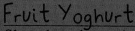

Fruit Yoghurt
Shop-bought yoghurts are often high in sugar and low in fruit so make your own healthy versions by stirring fresh fruit purée (see above) into thick plain bio or live yoghurt.

Mini Crumbles
Preheat the oven to 180°C (350°F/ Gas 4). Sprinkle 2 tbsp of the crumble mixture from p.102–103 over 3 peaches or nectarines (halved and stoned). Place the fruit on a baking dish. Pour a little water into the dish to prevent the fruit drying out. Cook in the oven for 20 minutes.

Homemade Fruit Spread

Put 110g (4oz) ready-to-eat dried apricots and 110g (4oz) ready-to-eat dried dates in a saucepan with 425ml (15fl oz) water. Bring to the boil, reduce the heat, cover and simmer for 45 minutes. Transfer to a blender, add 5 tbsp of water and blend to a purée. Store in a jar in the fridge for up to 1 week.

Chocolate Banana

Preheat the oven to 180°C (350°F/ Gas 4). Slice a banana lengthways, but not all the way through. Press cubes of chocolate into the gap and then wrap the banana in a foil. Bake for 20 minutes, until the chocolate has melted.

Popcorn

Pour 1 tbsp sunflower oil into a medium saucepan. Heat the oil then add a thin layer of popcorn (one kernel deep). Put the lid on the pan and cook over a medium heat, shaking the pan occasionally, until the corn has popped. Caution – don't remove the lid until the sound of popping has stopped!

Warm Fruit Salad

Cook your favourite dried fruits in a little water over a low heat for about 20 minutes, or until soft and plump. Add a cinnamon stick and a little ground nutmeg if you like and serve with natural yoghurt.

Banana Ice Cream

Wrap a peeled banana in cling film. Freeze for about 2 hours or until solid then remove the cling film and whiz in a food processor until roughly chopped. Serve in a bowl with a drizzle of maple syrup and a sprinkling of nuts.

• **Preparation** 10 mins • **Cooking** none • **Serves** 4–6

Melon Fruit Bowl

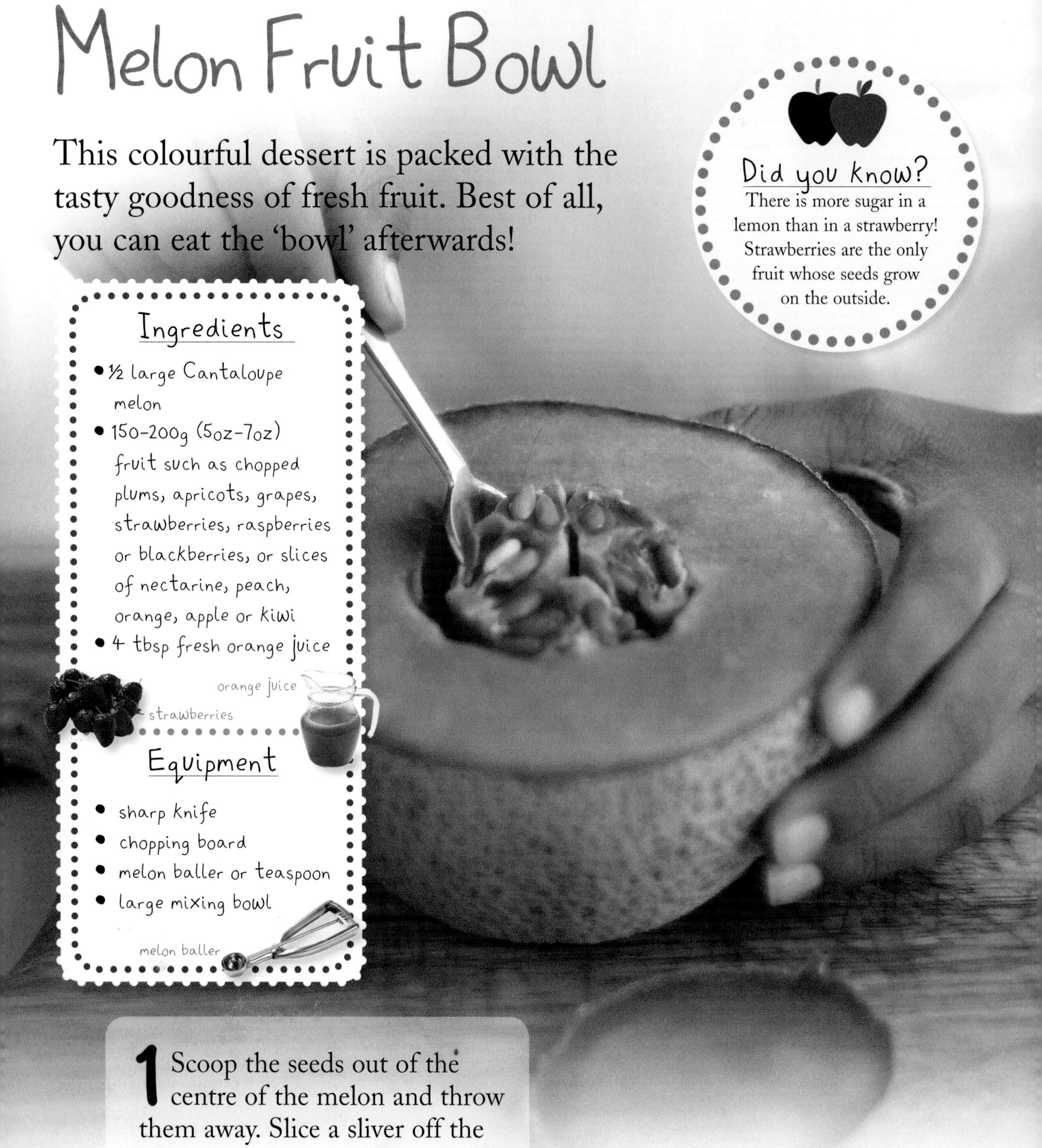

This colourful dessert is packed with the tasty goodness of fresh fruit. Best of all, you can eat the 'bowl' afterwards!

Did you know?

There is more sugar in a lemon than in a strawberry! Strawberries are the only fruit whose seeds grow on the outside.

Ingredients

- ½ large Cantaloupe melon
- 150–200g (5oz–7oz) fruit such as chopped plums, apricots, grapes, strawberries, raspberries or blackberries, or slices of nectarine, peach, orange, apple or kiwi
- 4 tbsp fresh orange juice

strawberries

orange juice

Equipment

- sharp knife
- chopping board
- melon baller or teaspoon
- large mixing bowl

melon baller

1 Scoop the seeds out of the centre of the melon and throw them away. Slice a sliver off the base of the melon so it stands up and place it on a serving plate.

Food Facts

Melons, especially those with an orange flesh, contain plentiful amounts of beta carotene. This is necessary for good vision, healthy skin, and growth. Vitamin C is also found in this juicy fruit.

melon

2 Use a melon baller or teaspoon to scoop out most of the melon flesh. Leave an even 1cm (½in) border in your hollowed out bowl shape.

3 Prepare the rest of the fruit by washing, peeling, slicing and deseeding as appropriate. Mix with the orange juice and melon balls in a large bowl.

4 Fill the melon bowl with the fruit salad and then pour over any juice. Serve immediately for the freshest taste and maximum amount of vitamins.

Tropical Yoghurt Ice

Bursting with vitamins from the fresh fruit, this cool and creamy yoghurt ice is a healthy alternative to ice cream. Natural bio yoghurt has a smooth, creamy taste but is much lower in fat than cream. It contains beneficial bacteria that are good for your digestive system and is also rich in calcium.

Tasty Twists
Strawberries, plums, nectarines, raspberries and peaches taste just as good as the mango and banana. You will need about 450g (1lb) fruit.

Did you know?
More than 50% of the world's mangoes are grown in India. Mangoes belong to the same family as the cashew, pistachio and poison ivy.

Ingredients
- 2 medium ripe mangoes
- 2 medium bananas (peeled)
- 500g (1lb 2oz) thick natural bio yoghurt
- 3 tbsp icing sugar
- squeeze lemon juice

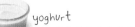
yoghurt

bananas

Equipment
- sharp knife
- chopping board
- blender or food processor
- spoon
- plastic container with lid
- whisk or fork
- ice cream scoop

ice cream scoop

1 To prepare each mango, cut away the two sides close to the stone. Taking the two large slices, cut the flesh into a criss-cross pattern down to the skin.

2 Press each mango half inside out and carefully cut off the cubes of mango. Cut away any remaining mango near the stone. Repeat with the second mango.

3 Break or slice the bananas into chunks and put them into a blender. Then add the mango, yoghurt, sugar and a squeeze of lemon juice.

Remove the ice cream from the fridge 30 mins before you want to eat it.

4 Blend until the mixture becomes thick and creamy. Pour the mixture into a shallow container, securely attach the lid and put it into the freezer.

5 After 2–3 hours whisk the mixture with a fork to break down any ice crystals. Freeze and repeat after 3 hours to give the yoghurt ice a creamy texture.

Food Facts

Mangoes are rich in vitamin C and beta carotene, and are a good source of vitamins A and B. However, these nutrients are greatly reduced when the mangoes are cooked.

mangoes

Peach and Orange Lollies

These refreshing ice lollies only take a few minutes to make and are a fun way to introduce fruit into your diet. Add thick natural yoghurt to make a frozen yoghurt lolly.

Did you know?
Peaches are the state fruit of South Carolina in the USA, while Georgia is known as the 'Peach State'.

Ingredients

- 3 ripe peaches or nectarines
- 300ml (10fl oz) fresh orange juice
- 1–2 tbsp icing sugar
- 4 heaped tbsp tinned fruit salad in natural juice, drained (optional)

glacé cherries

orange juice

Equipment

- small sharp knife
- chopping board
- large slotted spoon
- 2 bowls
- blender
- 4 ice lolly moulds

lolly moulds

1 Peaches can be tricky and messy to peel so here is a simple way to do it. Using a slotted spoon, lower the fruit into a bowl of boiling water.

2 After about 30 seconds, remove the fruit and then immediately plunge it into a bowl of cold water. The skin should peel away easily.

Tasty Twists

You could layer different fruits such as berries, mangoes, kiwis, oranges or bananas but you must partially freeze each layer for 45 minutes before adding the next or they will all mix together.

3 Carefully slice the fruit away from the stone and put it into a blender. Add the orange juice and 1 tablespoon of the icing sugar.

4 Blend the peaches, orange juice and icing sugar until smooth and frothy. Taste the juice and add the rest of the icing sugar if necessary.

Food Facts

Peaches are full of vitamin C and are also a good source of potassium and fibre. They contain beta carotene, which the body converts to vitamin A. Nectarines are a smooth-skinned variety of peaches.

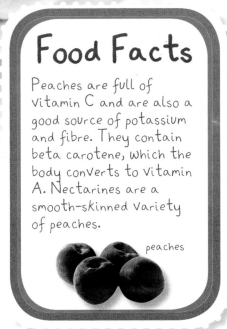

peaches

5 Spoon half of the fruit salad into the 4 moulds. Pour the juice over each mould until it is half full. Add the rest of the fruit salad and top up with fruit juice.

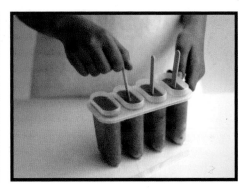

6 Insert the stick into the mould then freeze for at least 6 hours. Before eating, take the lollies out of the freezer and let them soften slightly.

Sunshine Jelly

Even though this healthier version of jelly is made with fruit juice and fresh oranges, it still contains sugar and should only be eaten as an occasional treat.

Tasty Twists

Mango, nectarine, peach or cherry would all taste great in this recipe, but any fruity flavours of jelly would work well.

Did you know?

Jelly was first eaten in Ancient Egypt. In the UK jelly and ice cream is a popular dessert, especially for children.

Ingredients

- 2 oranges
- 1 x 85g packet vegetarian real fruit lemon jelly granules
- 100ml (7fl oz) fresh orange juice

oranges

Equipment

- small sharp knife
- plate or chopping board
- 600ml (1 pint) jelly mould or glass bowl
- jug
- serving plate

sharp knife

mixing bowl

1 Cut a thin slice off one end of an orange to help it stand up on a plate or chopping board. Carefully slice downwards to remove the skin and pith.

2 Cut the orange into thin, round slices. Arrange some of the orange slices on the base and sides of the jelly mould or glass bowl.

3 Pour the orange juice into a jug, add the jelly granules and carefully top up with boiling water to make 600ml (1 pint) in total.

4 Stir gently until the jelly granules dissolve. Carefully pour half of the warm liquid jelly into the jelly mould, on top of the orange slices.

5 Put the remaining orange slices on top of the jelly and then pour over the rest of the liquid jelly. Leave to cool, then chill for at least 6 hours to set.

Helpful Hint

Pineapple, kiwi, papaya, pawpaw and figs are not suitable for this recipe because they contain enzymes which break down the jelly and stop it from setting.

6 Place a serving plate on top of the mould and then carefully turn it over so the plate is underneath – the jelly should slip out easily on to the plate.

Food Facts

Like all citrus fruits, oranges are a great source of vitamin C and they are full of natural sweetness and taste. It's better to use freshly squeezed fruit juice rather than one made from concentrates because a lot of the nutrients are lost during the manufacturing process.

orange juice

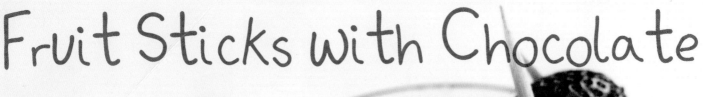

Fruit Sticks with Chocolate Orange Dip

This dessert is fun to make, and even more fun to eat! It is great for parties and works with any of your favourite fruits.

chocolate

Ingredients

- ½ cantaloupe melon (seeds scooped out)
- 1 small pineapple
- 3 kiwi fruit (peeled)
- 18 strawberries

Chocolate Orange Dip

- 150ml (5fl oz) milk
- 100g (3½ oz) milk or plain chocolate (broken into tiny pieces)
- zest of 1 orange (grated)

Equipment

- medium saucepan
- wooden spoon
- sharp knife
- chopping board
- melon baller or teaspoon
- 18 wooden cocktail sticks

strawberries

melon

melon baller

1 Pour the milk into a saucepan and add the grated orange zest. Bring the milk to the boil. Carefully, remove the pan from the heat, and add the chocolate.

2 Gently stir the milk until the chocolate has melted. Pour the sauce into a bowl and leave it to cool slightly while you prepare the fruit sticks.

Tasty Twists
Use any of your favourite fruits in this recipe. The Fruit Sticks taste equally delicious dipped into a yoghurt or fruit sauce (see p.86).

1 Top and tail the pineapple using a knife. Hold the pineapple upright on a chopping board and cut downwards to remove the skin.

2 Slice the pineapple and quarter each slice. Cut off the core and eyes. Halve the melon and scoop out the flesh in balls, with a melon baller or teaspoon.

3 Top and tail each kiwi fruit. Holding the fruit upright, slice downwards, away from you, to remove the skin. Then cut it into large chunks.

4 Thread some pineapple, a melon ball, a strawberry and a chunk of kiwi onto a cocktail stick. Repeat for all 18 sticks and serve with the chocolate dip.

Food Facts
A kiwi fruit has up to five times more vitamin C than an orange and is also a good source of fibre. You can even eat the kiwi fruit's skin!

kiwi fruit

Fresh or tinned pineapple is an excellent source of vitamin C as well as vitamin B1.

pineapple

Fruit Sundae

This fruity ice cream sundae is a refreshing, vitamin-filled treat. Any of your favourite fruits will taste great in this recipe and if you don't have time to make the Tropical Yoghurt Ice, you can use two extra scoops of vanilla ice cream instead.

Helpful Hints

Try to buy strawberries in season for the best, most nutritious fruit. The lemon juice enhances the flavour of the strawberries and also prevents the sauce oxidising or discolouring.

Ingredients

- 8 small scoops Tropical Yoghurt Ice (see p.90-91 for recipe)
- 4 small scoops Vanilla ice cream
- a selection of fresh fruit, such as strawberries, mango, kiwi fruit or raspberries (the amount depends on size of your glasses)
- toasted flaked almonds (optional)

Strawberry Sauce
- 350g (12oz) strawberries (hulled)
- squeeze of fresh lemon juice
- a little icing sugar

mango

raspberries

Equipment

kiwi

- sharp knife
- chopping board
- sieve
- blender or food processor
- ice cream scoop
- 4 sundae glasses

banana

⚠️

1 First make the Strawberry Sauce. Slice the strawberries in half and then purée them in a blender until they form a smooth sauce, with no lumps.

2 Press the strawberry purée through a sieve, using the back of a spoon, to remove the seeds. Stir in a little lemon juice and some icing sugar to sweeten.

3 Put a scoop of Tropical Yoghurt Ice into the glass and add a spoonful of Strawberry Sauce. Add some fruit and a scoop of vanilla ice cream.

4 Add more sauce and fruit and then top the sundae with a scoop of Yoghurt Ice and a sprinkling of nuts. Repeat to make three more sundaes.

Food Facts

Strawberries are a good source of vitamin C, which is excellent for your skin, hair and nails and also helps to boost your immune system.

strawberries

Fruity Apple Muffins

Tasty Twists
Instead of the English muffins, try raisin bread, brioche or currant buns. Alternatively, plain or fruit scones, bagels, pancakes or waffles taste great!

This recipe is perfect if you are looking to make a simple dessert but don't have much time on your hands. The apples can be peeled first if you prefer, but they are more nutritious with the skin on.

Serve the soft, golden apples on top of the eggy muffins. Delicious!

Ingredients

- 3 dessert apples
- 2 tsp lemon juice
- 2 tbsp unsalted butter (plus extra for cooking muffins)
- 2 tbsp soft light brown sugar
- ½ tsp ground nutmeg
- 2 free-range eggs (lightly beaten)
- 4 tbsp milk
- 4 cinnamon and raisin English muffins (halved)

English muffins

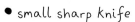
lighty beaten eggs

Equipment

- small sharp knife
- chopping board
- medium-sized bowl
- wooden spoon
- large frying pan
- tin foil
- tablespoon
- spatula
- shallow dish

shallow dish

large frying pan

1 Cut the apples into quarters and remove the cores. Cut the apples into thin slices. Put the slices in a bowl and add the lemon juice to coat the apples.

2 Melt the butter in the frying pan and then add the apple slices. Cook over a medium-low heat for 3–4 minutes, stirring frequently.

Food Facts

It is healthier not to peel the apples. Two-thirds of the fibre and lots of antioxidants are found in the skin. Antioxidants help to reduce damage to cells, which can trigger some diseases. Apples aid digestion and are said to be good for skin problems.

apples

3 Add the sugar and nutmeg and cook for another 1–2 minutes, until the apples have softened and the sauce turns golden and caramelises.

4 Remove the apples from the heat and put them in a bowl. Cover the bowl to keep the apples warm. Set aside while you prepare the muffins.

Did you know?
Charred apples have been found in prehistoric dwellings in Switzerland, showing that humans have been enjoying apples since at least 6500 BCE. Apples were also the favourite fruit of the ancient Greeks and Romans.

5 Put the eggs and milk into a shallow dish and mix them together. One by one, dip both sides of the muffin halves in the egg mixture.

6 Allow any excess egg mixture to drip off the muffins. Then melt a small knob of butter in a frying pan and swirl it around to coat the bottom.

7 Two at a time, put the muffins into the frying pan and cook each side for about 2 minutes or until the egg has set and they are light golden.

Oaty Crumble

Fruit crumble is one of the great British puddings. It is easy to make but tastes so good that it's very difficult to resist! Give this traditional dish a healthy twist by adding oats and seeds to the topping.

Tasty Twists

Try different varieties of fruit. Seasonal fruit tends to have the best flavour so in the summer months you could try nectarines, peaches, plums or rhubarb, and in late summer/early autumn try apples, blackberries or pears.

Ingredients

- 4 dessert apples
- 200g (7oz) blueberries (defrosted if frozen)
- 4 tbsp fresh apple juice
- 1 tbsp light muscovado sugar

Topping

- 75g (3oz) plain white flour
- 75g (3oz) wholemeal flour
- 75g (3oz) unsalted butter

(cut into small pieces)
- 75g (3oz) light muscovado sugar
- 3 tbsp sunflower seeds
- 1 tbsp sesame seeds
- 3 tbsp rolled oats

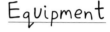
sunflower seeds

muscovado sugar

Equipment

- large mixing bowl
- small sharp knife
- chopping board
- spoon
- 900ml (2 pint) ovenproof dish
- small jug

sharp knife

mixing bowl

chopping board

1 Preheat the oven to 180°C (350°F/Gas 4). Put the plain white flour and wholemeal flour into a large mixing bowl and stir together with a spoon.

2 Add the butter. Rub the butter and flour together with your fingertips until they look like coarse breadcrumbs. Stir in the sugar, seeds and oats.

3 Remove the skin from the apples and cut them into quarters. Then carefully remove the core and slice the fruit into bite-sized pieces.

You can leave the skin on the apples, if you like – it is very good for you.

4 Put the pieces of apple into an ovenproof dish. Add the blueberries and pour over the apple juice. Sprinkle the sugar evenly over the top.

5 Spoon over the topping in an even layer then put the dish in the oven. Cook for 35 minutes until the top is crisp and beginning to brown.

Food Facts

For such a small fruit, blueberries pack a powerful health punch. According to recent research, they beat 40 other fruit and vegetables in helping to prevent certain diseases! They provide a high concentration of antioxidants which means they may help to prevent cancer and heart disease. What's more they may help to fight infections, boost memory and be anti-ageing.

blueberries

Fruit Bread Pudding

This is a quick version of the classic British dessert, summer pudding, which is usually made in a bowl and left overnight to allow the fruit juices to soak into the bread.

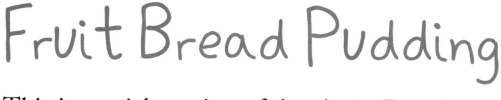

Did you know?

The word 'companion' comes from the Latin words 'com' meaning 'with' and 'panis' meaning 'bread' so it originally meant one with whom bread is shared.

Ingredients

stale wholemeal bread

blackberries

- 8 slices wholemeal bread (preferably slightly stale)
- 600g (1lb 5oz) mixed fresh or frozen berries such as strawberries, blackberries, blackcurrants and raspberries
- 125ml (4fl oz) water
- 100g (3½ oz) caster sugar

medium saucepan

strawberries

Equipment

sieve

- chopping board
- medium saucepan
- large pastry cutter or scissors
- bowl
- wooden spoon
- sieve
- large shallow dish
- tablespoon
- spatula or fish slice

wooden spoon

1 Cut the bread into your chosen shape using scissors or a large pastry cutter. (Use as much of the bread as possible to avoid waste.)

2 Put all but a handful of the berries, the water and about two-thirds of the sugar into a saucepan. Stir and then bring to the boil. Reduce the heat.

Food Facts

Bread is a staple food of many European, Middle Eastern and Indian cultures and is prepared by baking, steaming, or frying dough. There are more than 200 different types of bread but for the healthiest diet, you should try and eat wholegrain varieties which contain more fibre and B vitamins.

bread

3 Simmer the berries gently for about 7 minutes or until the fruit is soft and very juicy. Taste and add the remaining sugar if the fruit is too sharp.

4 Strain the juice from the fruit into a bowl. Press the fruit through a sieve into another bowl to make a purée. Throw away the seeds.

Tasty Twists

This delicious fruit purée would also taste great spooned over Banana Pancakes (see p.28-29), Tropical Yoghurt Ice (see p.90-91).

5 Place 4 bread shapes in a large shallow dish and spoon over the fruit purée until the bread is completely covered with the fruit.

6 Add a second piece of bread on top of the first. Spoon over the remaining purée and the berry juice. Gently press the bread with the back of a spoon.

7 Leave for at least 30 minutes to allow the bread to soak up the juice. Carefully lift out of the dish and decorate with the leftover berries and a little juice.

Apple Flapjacks

Preheat the oven to 180°C (350°F/ Gas 4). Over a low heat, melt 125g (4½oz) butter with 150g (5½oz) soft brown sugar and 3 tbsp golden syrup. Put 250g (8oz) porridge oats, 1 apple (cored and grated) and 2 tbsp sunflower seeds into a mixing bowl and stir in the butter mixture. Pour it into a greased 20cm (8in) square cake tin and bake in an oven for 20–25 minutes. Leave to cool and then cut into squares.

Baking

Shop-bought cakes and biscuits are usually high in sugar and fat. Many of the recipes in this section contain fruit whose natural sweetness helps to reduce the amount of refined sugar needed, as well as adding vitamins. Nutritious wholemeal flour is also used to add extra fibre and B vitamins. Here are a few suggestions to get you started.

Apple Tart

Preheat the oven to 180°C (350°F/Gas 4). Cut out 10cm (4in) circles of ready-rolled puff pastry. Arrange thinly sliced apples over the top, leaving a 1cm (½in) gap around the edge. Gently score the pastry around the fruit. Melt a little jam or honey in a small pan and brush it over the top of the apples. Place on a baking sheet and bake for 20–25 minutes, or until the pastry becomes golden.

Oaty Bread

Carbohydrate foods, such as oats, help to boost serotonin levels in the brain which make us feel happy. Here's how to adapt the roll recipe on p.122–123 to make a loaf of bread: Replace 50g (12oz) of the wholemeal bread flour with 50g (12oz) oats in step 2. In step 6 make 1 large loaf instead of 10 rolls and sprinkle the loaf with oats before baking it in step 7.

Savoury Scones

Preheat the oven to 220°C (425°F/ Gas 7). Sieve 110g (4oz) each of wholemeal and white self-raising flour and ½ tsp salt into a bowl. Rub in 50g (2oz) butter until the mixture looks like breadcrumbs. Make a well in the centre and pour in 150ml (5fl oz) milk. (If you like add 50g/2oz of cheese, sun dried tomatoes or ham.) Mix together to form a sticky dough and turn out onto a floured surface. Knead lightly until the dough is smooth and shape it into a circle about 2.5cm (1in) thick. Cut into smaller circles and brush the tops with milk. Place on a greased baking sheet and bake for about 20 mins.

Open Sandwich

Bread does not have to be made with wheat flour – you could use spelt flour, rye, corn flour or buckwheat. Try an open sandwich with a new type of bread. Experiment with toppings such as lettuce, cottage cheese and ham.

Fruity Muffins

Fresh and dried fruit add both sweetness and vitamins to your baking. On p.108– 109 you could stir 125g (4oz) of your favourite fruits such as apples, bananas, apricots or blueberries and raspberries into the mixture in step 4, instead of the dates.

Flatbread

This flatbread makes a great sandwich wrap. Put 175g (6oz) wholemeal self-raising flour and ½ tsp salt into a bowl. Stir in 1 tbsp vegetable oil and 120ml (4fl oz) water to make a soft dough. Knead on a lightly floured surface and put the dough into a lightly oiled bowl. Cover with cling film and leave for 1 hour. Then, divide the dough into 8 pieces and roll each one into circles, about 2mm (1/12 in) thick. Heat a lightly oiled, non-stick frying pan and cook for about 1½ minutes on each side, until golden and puffy.

Seed Rolls

Nuts and seeds give breads, biscuits and cakes a delicious taste and texture as well as adding important nutrients. For example, in step 3 of the roll recipe on p.122–123, try adding 5 tbsp of chopped nuts and seeds instead of sprinkling sunflower seeds on the top.

Sticky Date Muffins

These muffins taste light and luscious! The secret to good muffins is to not over-beat the batter otherwise they will be heavy and dense. For the perfect muffins give the mixture a gentle stir with a wooden spoon until the flour just disappears.

Did you know?
Dates are the fruit of the date palm tree, which can grow up to 25 metres (82 feet) tall. Egypt is the world's largest producer of dates.

Ingredients

caster sugar

egg

- 200g (7oz) white or wholemeal plain flour
- 1 tbsp baking powder
- 125g (4oz) caster sugar
- 1 tsp ground cinnamon
- ½ tsp salt
- 125g (4oz) ready-to-eat dried chopped dates
- 1 tbsp orange juice
- 175ml (6fl oz) milk
- 1 large egg (lightly beaten)
- 140g (5oz) butter

ground cinnamon

wholemeal flour

Equipment

blender

- large muffin tin
- sieve
- large mixing bowl
- wooden spoon
- food processor or blender
- small saucepan
- jug　　● fork
- wire rack
- paper cases

large muffin tin

1 Preheat the oven to 200°C (400°F/Gas 6). Line the muffin tin with the paper cases. Sieve the flour and baking powder into a bowl.

2 Stir the sugar, cinnamon and salt into the flour and baking powder. Put the dates and orange juice in a blender and whiz until they form a smooth purée.

3 Melt the butter in a saucepan over a low heat. Pour the milk into a jug and add the egg, melted butter and date purée. Beat together lightly with a fork.

Tasty Twists

Fresh fruit such as blueberries, raspberries and strawberries make a delicious alternative to the puréed dates. Alternatively, try other dried fruits such as raisins, cherries, apricots, cranberries or prunes.

Food Facts

Dates are one of the oldest cultivated fruits in the world and have been around since about 6000 BCE. They are soft and tasty and a natural sweetener. Dates are also a good source of iron, fibre and potassium as well as being low in fat.

dates

4 Pour the date mixture into the flour mixture. Fold the ingredients together gently and evenly with a wooden spoon until the flour is just mixed in.

5 Spoon the mixture into the paper cases until it is almost to the top. Bake for 20 minutes until risen and golden. Transfer the muffins to a wire rack to cool.

Passion Cake

With no creaming or whisking, this is a deliciously simple cake recipe. Carrots give the cake a light and moist texture, as well as providing essential nutrients.

Helpful Hints

To test the cake is cooked, insert a metal skewer into its centre. If it comes out clean, without cake mixture sticking to it, the cake is ready to take out of the oven.

Decorate the cake with slivers of orange peel.

Ingredients

self-raising wholemeal flour

- butter (for greasing)
- 125g (4½ oz) wholemeal self-raising flour
- 125g (4½ oz) white self-raising flour
- 2 tsp ground mixed spice
- 250g (9oz) light muscovado sugar

free-range eggs

- 250g (9oz) carrots (peeled and grated)
- 4 free-range eggs
- 200ml (7fl oz) sunflower oil
- 125g (4½ oz) reduced-fat cream cheese
- 1 tsp vanilla extract
- 5 tbsp icing sugar

Equipment

- 20cm (8in) square cake tin
- baking paper
- sieve
- large mixing bowl
- wooden spoon
- measuring jug
- skewer
- palette knife

measuring jug

sieve

1 Preheat the oven to 180°C (350°F/Gas 4). Lightly grease a 20cm (8in) square cake tin and then carefully line the base with baking paper.

2 Sieve both types of flour into a bowl, adding any bran left in the sieve. Stir in the mixed spice, sugar and carrots until they are thoroughly combined.

3 Crack the eggs into a jug. Use a fork to lightly beat them together. Then pour the eggs into the bowl with the flour mixture.

4 Add the oil and then stir until all the ingredients are mixed together. Pour the mixture into the tin and smooth the top with the back of a spoon.

Food Facts

Not all fats are bad (see p.14–15). Vegetable oil is a type of unsaturated fat which is a good source of energy and helps your body to absorb some vitamins.

vegetable oil

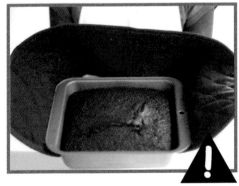

5 Bake the cake for 50 minutes until it is risen and golden. Remove it from the oven and leave to cool in the tin for 10 minutes before turning it out.

6 Carefully turn the cake out on to a cooling rack. Put the cream cheese and icing sugar into a bowl and beat together until smooth and creamy.

7 Stir in the vanilla extract. Put the icing in the fridge for 15 minutes to harden slightly. Spread the icing over the cake and smooth using a palette knife.

Fruity Flapjacks

Traditional flapjacks are healthier than many
other desserts because of the oats.
These ones are even better
for you because of
the fruity layer in
the middle.

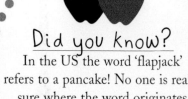

Did you know?
In the US the word 'flapjack'
refers to a pancake! No one is really
sure where the word originates
from although it does appear in
Shakespeare's play *Pericles* in
the early 17th century.

Ingredients

- 225g (8oz) ready-to-eat dried apricots
- 2 tbsp water
- 285g (10 oz) wholemeal flour
- 150g (5½ oz) porridge oats
- ½ tsp salt
- 200g (7oz) unsalted butter
- 110g (4oz) muscovado sugar
- 2 tbsp golden syrup

muscovado sugar

unsalted butter

golden syrup

Equipment

- scissors
- food processor or blender
- tablespoon
- large mixing bowl
- wooden spoon
- medium saucepan
- 18cm (7in) square cake tin
- baking paper
- palette knife

palette knife

square cake tin

scissors

112

1 Preheat the oven to 200°C (400°F/Gas 6). Grease and line the bottom of the cake tin with baking paper. Add the apricots and water to a blender.

2 Process the apricots until they are a purée. Set aside. Put the flour, oats and salt in a mixing bowl and stir with a wooden spoon until combined.

Food Facts

Both oats and dried apricots are high in soluble fibre, which helps to control blood sugar levels and keep energy levels steady. Dried apricots are also a good source of stamina-boosting iron.

oats

dried apricots

3 Melt the butter, sugar and syrup in a saucepan over a low heat. Stir the mixture occasionally until the butter has completely melted.

4 Pour the butter mixture into the mixing bowl containing the flour, oats and sugar. Stir until everything is combined in a sticky, oaty mixture.

Tasty Twists

You could use fresh fruit purée instead of dried. Raspberries, plums, blueberries or blackberries would all taste great. (See p.86.)

5 Press half of the mixture into the bottom of the cake tin and smooth it to make an an even layer. Carefully spread the apricot purée over the oaty layer.

6 Press the rest of the oaty mixture over the apricot purée until it is covered. Bake for 25–30 minutes or until the flapjack is golden on top.

7 Remove from the oven and leave to cool for 5 minutes. Divide the flapjack into squares and leave it to cool completely in the tin before turning it out.

Fruit and Nut Cookies

These yummy cookies are full of energy-boosting ingredients such as oats, dried fruit and nuts. They are much healthier than shop-bought ones, and taste better too!

⚠️ Nut allergy sufferers should leave out the nuts. The recipe will work just as well without them.

cranberries

Ingredients

- 75g (2¾ oz) dried apricots
- 100g (3½ oz) plain flour (wholemeal or white)
- 60g (2oz) whole porridge oats
- 50g (1¾ oz) chopped hazelnuts (optional)
- 125g (4½ oz) unsalted butter
- 75g (2¾ oz) soft light brown sugar
- 2 tbsp runny honey

apricots

honey   raisins

Equipment

- 2 baking trays
- scissors
- mixing bowl
- wooden spoon
- sharp knife
- small saucepan
- dessert spoon
- cooling rack

scissors

1 Preheat the oven to 180°C (350°F/Gas 4) and lightly grease 2 baking trays with butter. Cut the apricots into small pieces and put them in a mixing bowl.

2 Add the flour, oats and hazelnuts to the bowl. Mix together with a wooden spoon. Cut the butter into small chunks and put into a saucepan.

3 Add the sugar and honey to the saucepan. Heat them over a low heat. Stir gently with a wooden spoon, until the butter and sugar have melted.

4 Add the butter mixture to the bowl and mix. Put 5 dessert spoonfuls of the cookie dough onto each baking tray, leaving space between each one.

5 Flatten the cookies a little so they are about 5cm (2 in) diameter and 1cm (½ in) thick. Bake for 15 minutes or until they are light golden.

Tasty Twists

Chopped dried cherries, raisins, cranberries, peaches or dates can be used instead of apricots and any other nuts, such as walnuts, can be used instead of hazelnuts.

6 Remove the trays from the oven and leave the cookies to cool slightly. Then transfer the cookies to a cooling rack to cool and become crisp.

Food Facts

Flour is made by grinding grain, usually wheat. Wholemeal flour is made from the whole wheat grain with nothing added or taken away. It is higher in fibre and B vitamins than white flour, which is refined and processed until only about 75% of the grain is left. B vitamins are essential for producing energy, while fibre helps your digestive system work more efficiently.

wheat

Cherry and Apple Pies

Cherries and apples are combined in this variation of the American classic. This type of pie is called a free-form pie because it is not cooked in a dish and the sides of the pastry are simply gathered up to encase the filling.

Helpful Hint

Ground almonds, semolina or fine polenta help to soak up the fruit juices and prevent the pastry from going soggy. Ground almonds also add extra flavour but nut allergy sufferers should use semolina or fine polenta instead.

Ingredients

- 75g (2½ oz) unsalted butter (plus extra to glaze)
- 2 tbsp caster sugar
- 1 large egg (lightly beaten)
- 220g (7½ oz) plain flour (plus extra for dusting)
- 1 tbsp water

Filling

- 2 tbsp caster sugar
- 300g (10½ oz) pitted tinned cherries (drained weight)
- 2 dessert apples
- 50g ground almonds, semolina or fine polenta

dessert apples

Glaze

- 1 large egg (lightly beaten)

Equipment

- 2 large baking sheets
- baking paper
- scissors
- mixing bowl
- food processor or blender
- cling film
- sieve
- vegetable peeler
- rolling pin

cling film

food processor

1 Line the baking sheets. Put the butter, 75g (3oz) of the sugar and 1 egg into a food processor and process until smooth and creamy.

2 Add the flour and 1 tablespoon of water to the processor and whiz until the mixture comes together in a ball. (The pastry will be quite soft.)

Did you know?
Perhaps rather appropriately, cherries date back to the Stone Age. Cherry stones have been found in many Stone Age caves in Europe.

3 Turn the dough out on to a lightly floured work surface and gather it until it forms a smooth ball. Cover with cling film and chill for 30 minutes.

4 Preheat the oven to 200°C (400°F/Gas 6). While the pastry is chilling, drain the cherries in a sieve and mix with the apples, sugar and almonds.

Food Facts

Tinned fruit is used in this recipe because cherries are seasonal and therefore only widely available at certain times of the year. Choose fruit tinned in natural juices rather than with added sugar or syrup.

tinned cherries

5 Divide the pastry into 6 pieces. On a lightly floured surface, roll the pastry into thin circles about 13cm (5in) in diameter. Put on the baking sheet.

6 Brush the pastry with egg and sprinkle on the almonds. Add the fruit leaving a 2.5cm (1in) border. Gently gather the pastry to make open-topped pies.

7 Brush the outside of the pies with egg. Place a small piece of butter on top of the fruit. Bake the pies for 25 mins or until the pastry is light golden.

Raisin Soda Bread

Soda bread is the perfect starting point for anyone who hasn't made bread before. It doesn't contain yeast so it doesn't need as much kneading or rising as ordinary bread, but it's every bit as tasty.

If the dough is too dry in step 4, add a little extra buttermilk.

Helpful Hints
If you can't find buttermilk in the shops, use the same quantity of low fat natural yoghurt or milk combined with 1 tablespoon of lemon juice.

Ingredients

- 200g (7oz) wholemeal plain flour
- 200g (7oz) white plain flour (plus extra for dusting)
- 1 tsp salt
- 1 tsp bicarbonate of soda
- 50g (2oz) porridge oats
- 1 heaped tbsp caster sugar
- 125g (4½ oz) raisins
- 1 egg (lightly beaten)
- 300–350ml (10–12fl oz) buttermilk

raisins

wholemeal plain flour

Equipment

wooden spoon

- baking sheet
- sieve
- jug
- large mixing bowl
- wooden spoon
- knife

large mixing bowl

Food Facts

Traditionally, buttermilk is the liquid remaining after the cream has been churned into butter. It is low in fat and is often used to make pancakes and scones as well as soda bread. When combined with bicarbonate of soda it acts as a raising agent. Remember, if you can't get buttermilk, natural yoghurt is a great alternative.

buttermilk

Tasty Twists

Chopped dried dates, cranberries, blueberries or cherries could be used instead of raisins – or you could try a mixture of dried fruits.

1 Preheat the oven to 200°C (400°F/Gas 6). Sprinkle a baking sheet with flour until it is lightly covered. This will prevent the loaf sticking to the sheet.

2 Sieve the wholemeal and white flour, salt and bicarbonate of soda into a mixing bowl. If there is any bran left in the sieve, add it to the bowl.

3 Add the oats, sugar and raisins to the bowl and stir. Make a well in the centre of the mixture and pour in the egg and 300ml (10fl oz) of the buttermilk.

4 Mix together with a wooden spoon. When the mixture starts to come together, use your hands to form a soft, slightly sticky ball of dough.

5 Put the dough onto a lightly floured work surface and gently knead, once or twice, until the dough is smooth. Don't over-knead or the dough will toughen.

6 Form the dough into a flattish circle, about 18cm (7in) round and 4cm (1½ in) thick. Put the dough on the floured baking sheet.

7 Sieve over a little extra flour. Cut a large, deep cross, almost to the bottom of the dough. Bake for 30–35 minutes, or until risen and golden.

Banana and Pineapple Cake

This rich, moist cake is the tastiest fruit cake around! It is the perfect addition to a picnic or school lunchbox or it makes a great after dinner treat.

Did you know?
Banana plants have been in around for a long time. One of the first records dates back to Alexander the Great's conquest of India where he first discovered bananas in 327 BCE!

Ingredients

 self-raising wholemeal flour

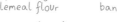 bananas

- 125g (4oz) unsalted butter, cut into small pieces (plus extra for greasing)
- 5 small bananas (about 450g/1lb peeled weight)
- 75g (3oz) ready-to-eat dried pineapple
- 175g (6oz) self-raising white flour
- 50g (2oz) self-raising wholemeal flour
- 1 tsp baking powder
- pinch of salt
- 125g (4oz) unrefined caster sugar
- 2 large free-range eggs
- 50g (2oz) chopped walnuts (optional)

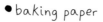 free-range eggs

Equipment

 scissors

- 900g (2lb) loaf tin
- baking paper
- small bowl
- fork
- scissors
- sieve
- large mixing bowl
- wooden spoon

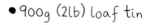 mixing bowl

loaf tin

1 Preheat the oven to 180°C (350°F/Gas 4). Trace around the loaf tin onto baking paper and cut it out Lightly grease the tin with butter and then line.

2 Put the bananas in a bowl and mash them with a fork. Cut the pineapple into very small pieces. Set the bananas and pineapple aside.

Helpful Hint

If the pineapple is very dry, it's best to soak it in hot water for about 1 hour or until it is tender.

3 Sieve the flour, baking powder and salt into a mixing bowl. Stir and then add the butter. Rub the butter into the flour mixture until it looks like fine breadcrumbs.

4 One at a time, crack the eggs into a small bowl. Lightly beat the eggs together with a fork until the whites and yolks are mixed together.

Food Facts

Pineapple is great for a sensitive stomach because it contains an enzyme called bromelain which is anti-inflammatory. It helps to reduce swelling and aids speedy recovery from surgery. It also aids digestion.

pineapple

5 Pour the beaten eggs into the mixing bowl, add the sugar, bananas and pineapple and mix together. Pour the cake mixture into the prepared loaf tin.

6 Make sure the mixture is level and then sprinkle over the walnuts. Cook in the centre of the oven for about 50 minutes until risen and golden.

7 Remove from the oven and place on a cooling rack for 10 minutes. Carefully turn the cooled cake out of the tin, cut into slices and serve.

Sunflower Seed Rolls

There's nothing like the aroma of fresh bread! All you need is a handful of basic ingredients to make these seedy rolls. You could also make a single loaf instead of the rolls (see p.106).

(see p.106)

Tasty Twists

Instead of sprinkling the seeds over the top of the rolls, you could mix them into the dough in step 2. Sesame, pumpkin or poppy seeds also taste great.

To test if the rolls are cooked, lightly tap the base – if it sounds hollow, it is cooked!

Ingredients

- 350ml (12fl oz) tepid water
- 2 tsp dried yeast
- 50g (12oz) strong white bread flour
- 150g (5½ oz) strong wholemeal bread flour
- 1½ tsp salt
- 1 egg (beaten)
- 5 tbsp sunflower seeds

sunflower seeds

wholemeal bread flour

Equipment

- small bowl
- large mixing bowl
- wooden spoon or tablespoon
- baking sheets
- pastry brush
- jug

mixing bowl

wooden spoon

1 Pour 100ml (3½ fl oz) of the water into a small bowl. Sprinkle in the yeast and stir until dissolved. Set aside for 5 minutes.

2 Put both types of flour and the salt into a large mixing bowl and mix together. Make a well (a large hole) in the centre of the flour.

3 Pour the yeast and most of the remaining water into the well and gently stir in the flour. Stir in the rest of the water, if necessary, to make a soft dough.

4 Turn the dough out on to a floured work surface. Knead for 10 minutes until smooth and shiny. Put the dough in a clean bowl and cover with a tea towel.

5 Leave to rise for 1½–2 hours, until it has doubled in size. Preheat the oven to 220°C (425°F/Gas 7). Knock back the risen dough with your knuckles.

6 Divide the dough into 10 pieces. Dust your hands with flour and shape the dough into rolls. Cover the rolls and set aside for 10 minutes.

7 Brush each roll with beaten egg and gently press the sunflower seeds into the tops. Bake for 25–30 minutes or until risen and golden.

Food Facts

Yeast is a single-celled micro-organism that is part of the fungus family and can be bought fresh or dried. It is used in bread-making to make the dough rise and give the bread a light, airy texture. To work, the yeast needs warmth and moisture. It ferments and produces tiny bubbles of gas which make the dough rise and give it a light, spongy texture.

fresh yeast

Glossary

This is the place to find extra information about the cookery words and techniques used in this book.

A

Additives – substances added to processed food to add colour, flavour or extend its shelf life.

Amino acids – proteins known as the 'building blocks of life' because they are necessary for the body to grow and repair itself. The body can make some itself, but others are obtained from food.

Antibodies – proteins made by the body's immune system to fight viruses or bacteria.

Anti-inflammatory – a property of a substance that reduces signs of inflammation such as swelling, heat, redness and pain.

Antioxidant – vitamins, minerals and phytochemicals that protect the body against the damaging effects of too many free radicals (which can damage the body's cells).

B

B Vitamins – a group of vitamins essential for the breakdown of carbohydrates, proteins and fats in the body. They are thiamin, riboflavin, niacin, B6, pantothenic acid, biotin, folic acid and B12.

Bake – to cook food in an oven. This uses dry heat (without liquid) and browns the outside of the food.

Beat – to stir or mix an ingredient quickly, to add air.

Beneficial bacteria – bacteria living in the intestines that that help to break down food and keep harmful bacteria from multiplying.

Beta carotene – the substance that gives orange and yellow fruit and vegetables their colour. It is converted by the body into vitamin A.

Bioflavonoids – compounds found in fruit and sweet vegetables. They help to maintain the health of blood capillaries.

Bland – describes food which has little flavour of its own.

Blend – to mix ingredients together by hand or in a blender or food processor to form a liquid or smooth mixture.

Blood sugar levels – the amount of sugar (glucose) in the blood. Bad diet can make this level rise and fall too quickly, causing health problems such as dizziness and mood swings.

Boil – to heat a liquid to a very hot temperature so that it bubbles and gives off steam.

Bran – husks of cereal grains that have been separated from the flour.

Brown – to cook food, usually by baking, frying or grilling, so that it becomes golden.

C

Calcium – a mineral essential for healthy bones and teeth. It also helps muscles and nerves to work properly.

Carbohydrates – food group that includes starchy and sugary foods. They are used by the body as a source of energy.

Carotenoids – pigments similar to carotene found in some plant foods.

Cholesterol – a fat mainly produced in the liver. Diets rich in saturated fats may lead to high cholesterol levels in the blood, increasing the risk of heart attacks and strokes.

Concentrated – when food has had non-essential ingredients, such as water, removed.

Cultivation – preparing soil for growing crops by digging it and removing weeds.

D

Deep-fry – to fry in a deep pan with a lot of oil so that the food becomes golden and crispy.

Digestion – the process by which the body breaks down foods that have been eaten so that they can be used for essential functions such as growth and repair.

Digestive system – the organs of the body through which food passes as it is being digested. They are the mouth, oesophagus, stomach and intestines. The liver and pancreas are also part of the digestive system as they secrete chemicals necessary for digestion.

Dough – a firm mixture of flour, liquid and usually other ingredients, that can be kneaded and shaped to make bread, rolls or pastry.

Dry fry – to fry without oil or fat.

E

Enzymes – proteins made from amino acids that spark off chemical reactions in the body. Each enzyme has a specific function, for example, lactase is an enzyme whose only function is to break down lactose in milk products.

F

Fats – food group that includes oils and hard fats such as margarine. Fats may be either saturated or unsaturated. Too many saturated fats can cause heart disease, whereas unsaturated fats generally help to prevent it.

Fatty acids – the main part of all fats, for example saturated, polyunsaturated and monounsaturated. The wrong balance of fatty acids can increase the risk of heart disease.

Fibre – the part of a plant food that is not digested, but passes through the digestive system and out of the body. Fibre is good for you because it helps to keep your bowels working properly.

Free-range – a word to describe farm animals that have been bred and kept in conditions where they are free to move around. It also describes the eggs of free-range hens.

Fry – to cook food over a direct heat in a frying pan or saucepan, using a little oil.

G

Germ – a tiny organism, only visible under a microscope, that is capable of invading the body and causing disease. Bacteria and viruses are germs.

Griddle – to cook food over heat on a special ridged pan that allows the fat to run away.

Grill – to cook or brown food under intense heat.

H

Husk – the outer covering of a seed or grain.

I

Immune system – the body's self-defense system, whose job is to fight infection and disease.

Iron – a mineral the body needs to make healthy red blood cells. If you don't get enough iron in your diet, your blood will not be able to deliver oxygen to your body efficiently.

K

Knead – to fold and press dough with your hands to make it smooth and stretchy. This strengthens the gluten (a protein) in the flour.

L

Lean – meat that is composed mainly of muscle, containing little fat.

Lycopene – and antioxidant vitamin that is plentiful in tomatoes and some other red fruit and vegetables, such as watermelon.

M

Magnesium – a mineral needed for many vital body functions. It helps to regulate the heartbeat, strengthen bones and maintain nerve function.

Marinade – usually a mixture of oil and other flavourings that meat, fish or vegetables may be soaked in before cooking.

Marinate – to soak meat, fish or vegetables in the above before cooking so that they absorb flavour and stay moist and tender.

Melt – to reduce a solid, such as butter, to a liquid using heat.

Micro-organism – an organism so small it can only be seen under a microscope.

Minerals – nutrients found in food that are essential to keep the body healthy. They are only needed in small amounts.

N

Nutrients – compounds contained within food that provide nourishment to the body. They include proteins, carbohydrates, fats, vitamins and minerals.

P

Phosphorus – an essential mineral that helps the cells in your body to function normally.

Phytochemicals – chemicals which come from plants. They are not strictly nutrients but they help your body to fight diseases and stay healthy.

Poach – to cook in gently simmering liquid. Eggs and fish are often poached.

Potassium – a mineral that is essential for growth and good health. Among other things it keeps your blood pressure normal and helps your muscles to work properly.

Protein – this comes from both plant and animal sources and helps your body to grow and stay healthy. Protein is made up of small components called amino acids.

Pureé – fruit, vegetables, pulses, meat or fish that are blended or liquidised (usually with liquid) to make a pulp.

R

Raising agent – a substance such as baking powder used to add air or gas to make food rise and become light and fluffy.

Refined – food that has been processed. Wholegrain foods are better for you because they have not been overly refined.

Roast – to cook food in the oven at a high temperature.

S

Sauté – to fry using oil or fat to brown food.

Season – to add salt and pepper to food to add flavour and bring out other flavours.

Selenium – a mineral that helps your immune system. It is also an antioxidant which protects your cells.

Shred – to cut or tear food into narrow strips.

Sieve – to put food through a mesh utensil (also called a sieve!) in order to remove lumps or coarse particles.

Slice – to cut food into thin or thick pieces, using a knife.

Staple food – the food which forms the main part of a community's diet. It is usually a carbohydrate food such as rice or potatoes.

Stir – to mix food in a circular motion, usually with a spoon.

Stir-fry – to fry food in a little oil over a high heat, stirring constantly.

T

Toast – to brown or crisp food, especially bread, using a toaster, grill or frying pan.

Toxin – a substance that has a negative effect on your body. It can enter your body in or on what you eat.

V

Vitamin A – also known as retinol, this vitamin helps maintain the health of your skin. It also strengthens immunity from infections and helps vision in dim light.

Vitamin C – also known as ascorbic acid, this vitamin protects your cells and helps your body to absorb iron from food.

Vitamin D – this helps to regulate the amount of calcium and phosphorus in your body.

Vitamin E – an antioxidant that helps protect cell membranes.

Vitamins – essential nutrients that your body needs to work properly and stay healthy.

W

Whisk – to briskly mix ingredients together using a fork or whisk in order to combine them and add air.

Z

Zinc – an element that helps your body to make new cells and enzymes. It also processes protein, fat and carbohydrates and helps to heal wounds.

Index